The World in 1492

By Jean Fritz, Katherine Paterson,
Patricia and Fredrick McKissack,
Margaret Mahy, and Jamake Highwater

With illustrations by Stefano Vitale

Henry Holt and Company • New York

Introduction copyright © 1992 by Henry Holt and Company, Inc.
"Europe in 1492" copyright © 1992 by Jean Fritz
"Asia in 1492" copyright © 1992 by Katherine Paterson
"Africa in 1492" copyright © 1992 by Patricia and Fredrick McKissack
"Australia and Oceania in 1492" copyright © 1992 by Margaret Mahy
"The Americas in 1492" copyright © 1992 by The Native Land Foundation
Illustrations copyright © 1992 by Stefano Vitale
All rights reserved, including the right to reproduce this book or portions
thereof in any form. Published by Henry Holt and Company, Inc.,
115 West 18th Street, New York, New York 10011.
Published simultaneously in Canada by Fitzhenry & Whiteside Ltd.,
91 Granton Drive, Richmond Hill, Ontario L4B 2N5.

Library of Congress Cataloging-in-Publication Data
The world in 1492 / by Jean Fritz . . . [et al.]; with illustrations
by Stefano Vitale. Includes bibliographical references and index.
Summary: Introduces the history, customs, beliefs, and accomplishments
of people living in Europe, Asia, Africa, Australia and Oceania, and the
Americas during the fifteenth century. ISBN 0-8050-1674-0
1. Fifteenth century—Juvenile literature. [1. Fifteenth century.
2. World history.] I. Fritz, Jean. II. Vitale, Stefano, ill.
D203.W67 1992909′.4—dc20 92-5434

Printed in the United States of America on acid-free paper. ∞

1 3 5 7 9 10 8 6 4 2

CONTENTS

INTRODUCTION

When we study world history, we usually read about people like Julius Caesar, Richard the Lionheart, and Copernicus. We seldom hear about the kingdoms of Africa, the great religions born in India, or the lively cultures of the Aboriginal Australians. When we study American history, we get the Pilgrims and Thomas Jefferson and the Civil War. We forget that American history goes back thousands of years before the coming of the Conquistadors.

Though the history of European civilization is a grand one, it's not the only one. There were also mighty civilizations in Asia, in Africa, and in the Americas. Great works of music, painting, poetry, and sculpture have been created by peoples everywhere. And all over the world, people have lived and died, playing their games and praying to their gods, handing down the timeless traditions. Their stories—their histories—are grand ones too. In *The World in 1492* you will read about some of these people.

Everyone knows that Columbus left Spain in 1492 hoping to reach the Far East by sailing west. But the story of Ferdinand, Isabella, and Columbus is not the only one of 1492. Across the Mediterranean, in Italy, the Renaissance was at its finest moment—Leonardo da Vinci was at the height of his genius, and a young man named Michelangelo Buonarroti was just beginning his career. And in that same year of 1492, back in Spain, Ferdinand and Isabella were casting out Spain's Moorish and Jewish populations.

How many people know that the China Columbus was hoping to find had, only a hundred years before, sent out its own explorers? Far larger and more numerous than Columbus's ships, the Ming fleet sailed thousands of miles and visited dozens of faraway seaports. By 1492 China had closed in on itself, having concluded that there was no point in exploring the unknown—everything worth knowing or having was already in China.

And what of Africa? In 1492, in the west African kingdom of Songhai, medical doctors were performing successful eye surgery. On the other side of the continent, in the marketplaces of the Swahili, fresh produce all the way from Indonesia could be purchased.

Who would guess that these same Indonesian islands also maintained trade with ports in Arabia, India, Melanesia, and China? In some ways they were the hub of the world. In Australia, and in the more remote islands of Polynesia, life in 1492 was much the same as it had been for hundreds, even thousands, of years. History was recorded not in written chronicles, but in stories, in songs, in legends—all too many of them now lost to us forever.

North and South America, like Australia and much of Oceania, were independent of the world of the Asians, the Africans, and the Europeans. What was life like for the people who had been living in the Americas for millennia?

It's difficult for us to imagine the Americas of five hundred years ago. There is much we simply do not know. The great Inca Empire, for instance, kept no written records; like the Australians, the Incas kept their histories in their heads. When four-fifths of the Incas died, whether from disease or by the sword, within ten years of first contact with the Conquistadors, their stories died with them.

We don't even have accurate names for many peoples and places. Following Columbus, we refer to the inhabitants of North and South America as Indians. Even in his lifetime, Columbus was nearly alone in his stubborn belief that he had reached the Indies. But somehow the name stuck. What are the alternatives? The phrase *Native American* is equally misleading—after all, the word *America* comes from the name of another Italian explorer, Amerigo Vespucci. *Amerindian* only doubles the problem.

There just isn't an ideal name in the English language—or in any language, really—to call these peoples. In 1492, the people of Australia did not call themselves Aborigines, which means "from the beginning." That would have been useful only in contrast to someone who *wasn't* there from the beginning. Five hundred years ago, the Aborigines were the only people living in Australia—there was no one to contrast them to. (It would be more fair to use Inaboriginal—"*not* from the beginning"—to describe Australia's later inhabitants.)

We speak of the peoples who lived in 1492 on the shores of Africa's Lake Victoria. But Queen Victoria, for whom the lake is named, was not born for another three hundred years. We refer to events as happening B.C. (before Christ) or A.D. (*anno Domini,* "in the year of the Lord"), using the year of Jesus' birth as the counting-down-to and -up-from point. Not everyone kept or keeps this system of dates. The Aztecs had a very complicated, accurate calendar based on a cycle of fifty-two years. The Islamic, Jewish, and Chinese calendars are still used by millions of people today.

We speak of "Indians" in the year "1492" because there's no better way for us to name those peoples and that moment in time. But we should keep in mind that the Aztecs (and the Incas, and the people of the Plains) did not call themselves Indians, and that it was the year 1492 only to Christians.

Five hundred years ago, Europeans did not represent the world's dominant culture. Europe was still recovering from the political chaos that followed the fall of the Roman Empire. Little more than a century before Columbus's birth, the bubonic plague had cut Europe's population by more than a third. By the standards of some African and Asian societies, European awareness of the wider world was poor. Even the best-educated Europeans had only the dimmest notion of African and Asian geography. They imagined the Indian Ocean as a large lake surrounded by land. Meanwhile, seagoing traders from East Africa, India, and the Far East were doing business with each other daily.

Everyone knows that Columbus, rather than reaching his intended destinations in Asia, "discovered" America in 1492. Soon enough, the age of European expansion—conquest, enslavement, colonization, conversion—began. In 1505 the Portuguese razed the Swahili port of Kilwa. In 1521 the Spanish sacked Tenochtitlán, capital of the Aztec Empire. By the beginning of the nineteenth century, British colonials had driven the people of Tasmania, an island off the southern coast of Australia, to extinction.

No, the story of Ferdinand, Isabella, and Columbus was not the only one. In *The World in 1492* you will read about other fascinating people, places, and events of the time. There are chapters on Europe, Asia, Africa, Australia and Oceania, and the Americas—personal essays on what each author felt were the most exciting aspects of his or her part of the world. They are not meant to cover everything. Not by any means are all the stories of 1492 included. When Columbus stops being the only story of 1492, more stories unfold than could possibly be contained in one book.

And that just may be the point.

The World

—IN—

1492

EUROPE IN 1492
Jean Fritz

If Christopher Columbus had been born one hundred or one hundred and fifty years earlier, he probably would never have thought of crossing the Ocean Sea. Certainly he would not have been able to convince any king or queen in Europe to finance such a foolish venture. In 1492, however, Europe was taking a giant step from one age into another, from what is now known as the medieval world into the modern world.

For a thousand years people in medieval Europe had considered themselves first and last as members of Christendom. They were determined to defend themselves from the expanding world of Muslims (followers of Muhammad), who lived in north Africa, in many parts of Asia, in Arabia, and in the greatest of all Muslim states, the Ottoman Empire. United as Christians, Europeans nevertheless fought among themselves, constantly rearranging boundaries that defined not only some of the nations we think of today, but countless subdivisions that no longer exist.

Yet in their thinking, most people kept strictly within the boundaries set by the church headed by the pope in Rome. Indeed, no matter what question a person might raise, there was just one authority—the Bible, which could be interpreted by the church and the church alone. An answer that could not be found in the Bible simply wasn't right. Besides, people were told that they should be preparing for the Day of Judgment, not asking questions or wasting their time being curious. And if anyone did express opinions that did not conform to those of the church, that person was put on trial for heresy. Beginning in the eleventh century, the church carried out trials known as the Inquisition. All over Europe, church Inquisitors spied on people suspected of heresy, questioned them (sometimes under torture), punished them, and frequently put them to death. Often the Inquisitors were accompanied by packs of black and white dogs, supposedly trained to sniff out the unfaithful. Nowhere was the Inquisition

Inquisitors order "Enemies of the Faith" to be burned at the stake.

more severe than in Spain. In 1481 three hundred heretics were burned to death, and during the next ten years three thousand more were burned.

Most Christians, however, were so firm in their faith that they saw nothing wrong in persecuting nonbelievers. But if anyone started persecuting them—watch out! They were particularly sensitive about the holy city of Jerusalem, which they had long been free to visit, despite its being ruled by Muslims since 627. But in the eleventh century, when the Muslims began to persecute Christian pilgrims and destroy their holy places, Christians rose up in arms. Men, women, children, knights, and peasants—all wearing the symbol of the White Cross—streamed across Europe in a cru-

sade to reclaim the holy city. There were nine crusades in all between the eleventh and the fourteenth centuries, but only the first was successful, and that one only temporarily: Jerusalem was captured but quickly lost again.

CONSTANTINOPLE FALLS TOO

The most devastating Muslim conquest, however, was made much later, in 1453, only two years after Christopher Columbus was born. The Ottoman Turks took the great city of Constantinople, which Christians considered their eastern capital just as Rome was their western capital. Europeans were horrified not only that another Christian citadel had fallen, but that a vital trading center had been taken from them.

Up to this time European traders had sent caravans from Constantinople on the long overland route to China to secure spices, jewels, and silks. Spices were particularly important to people in Europe. Ginger, pepper, and cloves were used not only to preserve meat but to disguise the taste of meat that was spoiling (and it often was!). Europeans were big meat eaters, but with the fall of Constantinople and the closing of the overland trade route, there would be no more spices.

Even more seriously, with no church in Constantinople, Christendom itself had shrunk. It seemed obvious that there was only one thing to do: fight! Medieval Europeans considered fighting a way of life, and the pope called for an immediate crusade—"the greatest of all wars," he called it. Still, not one European leader responded—not even the Holy Roman Emperor, who was crowned by the pope and was supposed to be responsible for all Christians.

Why not? Of course all Europeans wanted spices. Of course they didn't like Muslims acquiring more power. But now individual nations were becoming more powerful in their own right. Rulers were too busy fighting their own wars, involved in their own interests, to abandon everything for another crusade. The Holy Roman Emperor had his own problems. Although he was supposed to be an heir to the old Roman Empire, he ruled parts of what are now Germany, Switzerland, the Netherlands, and Austria. Yet all these areas were further subdivided, each subdivision with its own ruler

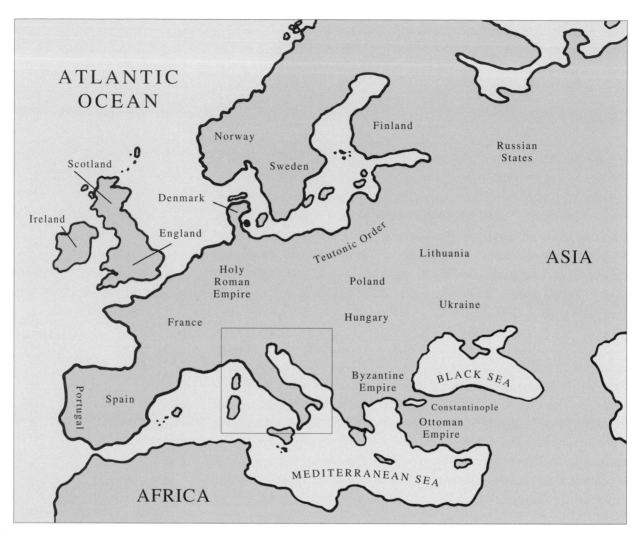

seeking to strengthen his own power. The Holy Roman Emperor didn't want to traipse off on a crusade that might be no more successful than the others had been.

THREE KINGS AND ONE QUEEN

Europe was changing. By the second half of the fifteenth century it had three exceptionally strong leaders moving toward a new era. The first, Louis XI of France (1423–83), came to his throne in 1461 and ruled for twenty-two eventful years filled with intrigue. A gawky man with rickety legs and a long, hooked nose, he inherited a kingdom that was on the verge of splitting into multiple sovereign districts ruled by nobles. That he brought them under control and asserted his authority endeared him to the common people but infuriated the nobles, who called him "the terrible king." He didn't allow the nobles to have fun—at least that's what they felt. Used to warring among themselves, they were forbidden to do so. Accustomed to hunting when they pleased, they couldn't go hunting without the king's permission. From time to time the nobles tried to resist, but without the help of the common people, they couldn't go far. Actually, Louis XI himself acted like a common person much of the time. He preferred to ride around the country without ceremony on a mule, to dress in cheap clothes, and to keep on his head an old felt hat that he loved. He consistently chose his friends and advisers from the middle class and often held meetings in public taverns rather than in his palace. Although France was slower than England to leave the medieval world, Louis XI left his nation on firmer ground than it had ever been, both politically and economically.

Louis XI of France.

In England, Henry VII (1457–1509) also reduced the power of his great nobles by excluding them from his Privy Council, the one arm of his government on which he relied. He replaced the nobles with clergy and lawyers, learned men who knew how to deal with practical affairs of state. Indeed, it was this reformed Privy Council that paved the way for Parliament to take its part later as the representative branch of the government. And it was the Star Chamber, the judicial branch of the Privy Council, that brought an unruly England to order. Henry VII, like Louis XI, was a strong administrator who developed commerce and industry. And as it happened, he turned out to be the richest king in Christendom.

Since the fall of the Roman Empire, Spain had been broken up into competing kingdoms, but when Isabella of Castile married Ferdinand of Aragon in 1469, Spain became a single nation for the first time. Like both Louis XI and Henry VII, Isabella (1451–1504) and Ferdinand (1452–1516) had to harness a restless aristocracy. Throughout Europe, however, they were most appreciated for fighting and vanquishing the Moors (Muslims from north Africa), who had occupied southern Spain for centuries. In 1492 Granada, the last Moorish stronghold, fell. A few months later, Isabella and Ferdinand, known as the Catholic Monarchs, evicted all non-Christians from Spain. These included not

Henry VII of England.

only the Moors but Jews, many of whom had been prominent scholars, astronomers, mathematicians, and doctors. While this mass eviction was taking place, Ferdinand and Isabella sent Christopher Columbus in search of China.

By unifying their countries, reducing the influence of warring noblemen, and elevating the working middle class, these rulers introduced to Europe the rudiments of the modern state. People were becoming conscious now of their national identity. They were proud of being different from other people, of developing their own variations in architecture, of favoring their own styles in dress and art. Although Latin (the language spoken by the ancient Romans) was still the "official" language of all Europe, particularly in universities and the church, more and more people were speaking and writing in their native languages. By the early 1400s public records, such as birth and death rolls, in England were kept not in Latin but in English. Diversity was acceptable; competition was in order. Europeans may have claimed that their first allegiance was to Christendom, but in fact many were primarily occupied with establishing the success and prosperity of their separate nations.

HOW PEOPLE LIVED IN THE FIFTEENTH CENTURY

But if Europe was embarking on major changes, the physical landscape looked much the same as it had for the last couple of centuries. There were still vast stretches of swampland, still forests spreading over the northern half of the land. Wolves, sables, and martins made their homes in these wild, lonely outposts. The southern landscape was tamer: vineyards in France, irrigated orchards in Spain, strips of green, cultivated fields, and on the plains and up the hillsides—sheep. They munched their lazy way over England and the continent—more sheep per square mile of countryside than people.

As for the people, there were about fifty-five million in Europe when Columbus was born. Fourteen million lived in France, three million in England. Those on farms were, for the most part, poor. They lived in small, smoky, one-room huts with walls of clay and straw, most with thatched roofs, except in Italy where the roofs were often tiled. Sometimes houses were extended so they could also shelter the animals. The people could look through a window

OPPOSITE: *Ferdinand and Isabella of Spain.*

and say goodnight to their ox and donkey (if that's what they had), and their ox and donkey could poke their heads through the window and watch the people eating. The people didn't mind. After all, the animals were their most precious possessions.

They treasured their beds, too. All people, rich or poor, had a special feeling for their beds, which were often a wedding gift from the groom's father. Rich people had feather beds with down comforters, sheets, bedspreads, and quilts, and sometimes canopies on top. Travelers compared notes on the beds in inns. German ones were the best. Not only were they comfortable, they had no lice. Poor peasants had to put up with lice and make do with straw mattresses, but they tried to discourage fleas by strewing mulberry leaves under them. But in spite of discomforts, all were proud of their beds, each so wide that it ruled the room. Indeed, since the whole family often slept in one bed, it had to be wide. The wider, the better. Otherwise, peasants generally owned nothing more than a table, bench, pot, salt cellar, five or six glasses, a pot for cooking peas, and a few farm implements. Their clothes hung on a bar along the wall: a tunic and long underwear for men, a chemise with removable sleeves for women. Both men and women had coats or cloaks, often fur-lined or fur-trimmed, with blue hoods for men in France and red for women.

THOSE NOISY CITIES!

There were more cities now than there had ever been, but as always they were circled by walls that seemed to be trying to contain the hustle-bustle inside. Sometimes, however, a city spilled over and houses hunkered down outside the walls. It may not have been as safe outside, but it was quieter. Cities were noisy places. High in the air the church bells rang and the tower clock chimed. Down below, wagon wheels clattered on narrow cobblestone streets, horses clumped, children shouted, vendors hawked their wares, street musicians sawed away at their fiddles, and from their balconies people yelled back and forth to one another. Indeed, the work and play of the city was carried out in an uproar.

Cities were also smelly. Garbage was thrown out windows, and since there were no inside toilets, waste was disposed of any-which-way, without regard for sanitation. As a result, people tried

OPPOSITE: *Peasants harvest grapes in a field. The building is a fanciful exaggeration of a medieval castle. From a fifteenth-century illuminated manuscript.*

Travelers pay a toll upon crossing a bridge. Etching based on a fifteenth-century stained-glass window.

to cover up the bad smells by wearing lots of perfume and by burning incense. Even mules were rubbed with perfume if they were to take part in a parade or festival. Venice, the richest city and one of the prettiest, was also one of the smelliest. Instead of streets, Venice had canals, and people dumped everything into them—but unfortunately not everything sank. German cities may have been the cleanest. Some of them even provided public baths and saunas. One city had thirty bath buildings—outdoor ones for common people, where men and women bathed and steamed together with only a fence between them. So popular were the baths that people often turned their bathing time into a party with meals served to them in the water.

THE POOR AND THE RICH

Common people, often called "little people," lived very differently from prosperous ones, or "fat people." As one Italian writer said: "One section of humanity is ill-treated to death so the other can stuff itself to the bursting point." Peasants depended on cereals and vegetables for their food, turnips and onions particularly, but also pork if they could afford to slaughter one of their pigs. But "fat people" really did stuff themselves, often on fantastic food— swans, herons, peacocks, for instance. Not even kings, however, were particular about *how* they ate. They might dine off gold plates, but they ate mostly with their fingers. Forks were very rare. Manners had not changed since the thirteenth century, when a book of etiquette advised people to wipe their mouths on the tablecloth after drinking. "Don't clean your ears with your fingernails while eating," the book said. "If you must spit, spit politely."

Some rich people, of course, were wealthier than others. The more money a family had, the more rooms in their home, the more servants, the more decoration, the fancier their gardens. Along the Mediterranean, slaves were common in the wealthy homes— Moors, Turks, and Russians bought in the process of trading.

But rich or poor, most people had dogs. The richer the family was, the more dogs they had. Dogs ran so wild in some country estates that a visitor to one estate remarked that the whole place smelled of dogs.

In the fifteenth and sixteenth centuries people loved their pets

Revelers gather for a feast. From a fifteenth-century illuminated manuscript.

so much that they often took them to church, especially in cold weather. Cats were encouraged to curl up on their mistresses' hands and keep them warm; dogs could be trained to sit on their masters' feet. Nuns were said to take pet birds to church on their shoulders, but since birds could not be expected to sit still for a service, this practice was discouraged. In warm countries caged birds hung on balconies; geese often patrolled the front gates, honking to alert their households to guests or strangers. Kings kept small zoos with perhaps a panther or two, an elephant, or even a giraffe acquired from trade with Africa.

But some things almost no one had. Glass for windows, for instance. Windows would be closed with wooden shutters or they

This 1517 woodcut depicts daily life in the French countryside.

might have translucent waterproof cloth stretched over them. Although cathedrals had stained-glass windows, only an occasional house had a single glass window, which would be pieced together from small round bits of glass joined by lead. Few people had mirrors, and no one had a bureau with drawers. For storage they used chests, sometimes piling one on top of another, sometimes lining them up around their beds.

No matter how well they lived, however, people had worries. Europe was a violent place, wars or no wars. Bands of robbers stalked the countryside and invaded cities, not only stealing as they went, but killing anyone who got in the way. Most people carried daggers or arms of some sort. And with good reason. In 1492 an average of fourteen people were murdered every day in Rome. In London few dared to go out at night, and even in the daytime a person never ventured alone into the countryside.

Sickness—that was another worry. Contagious diseases of all kinds spread like fire, but the worst came in the middle of the fourteenth century and was known as the Black Death because it produced black marks on the body. No one in Columbus's day remembered the Black Death, but all had grandparents or other ancestors who had been struck down. All knew the terrible stories. Forty percent of the population of Europe had been killed off in four years. Indeed, death moved so fast that the living could barely keep up with it. People with wheelbarrows would go through the streets crying: "Are there any dead? Bring out your dead." One Italian poet asked how future generations could be expected to believe the horror when those who had been there could hardly believe it. Still, there were reminders. The plague came back from time to time—not as severe, but who knew when it might strike them all down?

People lived in the midst of fear—if not of epidemics and violence, then of sin, magic, evil spirits. Terrible things could happen to people no matter how good they were, so it was no wonder that they tried to find ways to ward off evil and bad luck. Parents often tied pieces of coral around the necks of their children in the hope that this would protect them. They pierced the earlobes of their babies to keep them from having convulsions. People usually married on Sunday to bring them good luck, and many, kings included, consulted astrologers to make sure they were picking the best time to carry out their plans.

SCANDINAVIA AND RUSSIA

In many ways life in late fifteenth-century Europe was not much different from the way it had been for the last hundred years. What are now the Scandinavian countries—Norway, Sweden, Denmark—had become unified at the end of the fourteenth century; they squabbled with each other but generally left their southern neighbors alone. Switzerland, the most democratic country of all, had been a federation of self-governing regions for almost two hundred years and was known for being a peaceful nation, as it still is.

As for Russia, it was for the first time becoming a nation in its own right. Up to the time of Ivan III (1440–1505), whose reign began in 1462, Russia was made up of city states. These were subject to repeated attacks by the Tartars, tribes of Mongols and Turks who made their headquarters on a branch of the Volga River and collected tribute from Russian princes. Because of Tartar domination, Russians thought of themselves as in some ways more Asiatic than European. Yet it was the Russian Orthodox Church that gave them a common set of values and acted as a kind of mother to the people. The center of the church was in Moscow, which would become the capital of Russia. But Ivan III (Ivan the Great) was determined to end Tartar rule. And he did. In ten years, from 1470 to 1480, Ivan conquered one city-state after another and extended his rule to Finland, the Arctic, and the Ural Mountains. Then, with 150,000 men, he confronted the Tartars, staring them down across the Volga River until at last they retreated. Russia became an independent nation, owing tribute to no one.

Ivan III of Russia.

CHANGES CREEP IN

But it was primarily in England, France, Spain, and Italy where the greatest changes were taking place. In some ways change had begun as far back as the Crusades. To people who had never been far away from home, the Crusades opened up a whole new world. Christians met Muslims face to face and discovered that many of them were nice people—helpful and kind and learned. No traveler came home without having been exposed to new ideas. "In forty weeks of this pilgrimage," one crusader wrote, "a man learned to know himself better than in forty years elsewhere." Moreover, they began to ask questions. They had been used to accepting whatever the church taught them, but now they began to wonder. What about all those relics they were seeing? They had always revered relics associated with Jesus and the saints and displayed in churches—pieces of wood, for instance, from the Holy Cross. But now there were so many. They were shown hay from Jesus' manger, nails from his cross, the table from the Last Supper. And what were they to think when they came across the same relics time after time? One traveler reported seeing an arm of St. Thomas in three different places. "How many arms did St. Thomas have?" he asked.

The Crusades made some people more critical, more aware of viewpoints other than their own, but perhaps most important, Europe was for the first time projecting itself beyond its own borders, rubbing shoulders with alien cultures. Venice, for instance, which had always been in an ideal position to trade with the Arab world, was elevated by the Crusades to its glory. Indeed, Venice, along with Genoa, established such control over this trade that even after the fall of Constantinople, it was able to secure spices and silks from Egypt and Arabia and resell them at exorbitant prices to the rest of Europe. But woe unto any European ships that tried to muscle in on its trade!

The Black Death also accounted for changes in society. With the enormous labor shortage following the epidemic, peasants were less passive and had the opportunity to become craftsmen or tradesmen, and sometimes to own their own farms.

But it was the rise of strong kings that broke the power of old landholders, the barons who had created their personal realms, which in turn were dependent upon peasants. Yet the peasants in England wanted certain rights recognized. And so did the barons who were forced to knuckle under to kings, sometimes to such an arbitrary one as King John. In 1215 the rivalry between King John and the barons resulted in the signing of the Magna Carta, a document stating that the nobility did have certain privileges that even the king must respect. In addition, general grants were included to protect all subjects against oppression. This document may not have had much immediate effect, but it established the lasting ideas that government should be founded on law, and that individuals have rights. In the fifteenth century, while France was still

This 1568 woodcut shows printers operating an early press.

using torture to establish guilt or innocence, England had a jury system and a Parliament.

As trade increased and education spread, common people had a chance to get ahead, sometimes by hard work or because they had talent or perhaps because they had friends in high places. It is not known just how much formal education Christopher Columbus had. The son of a weaver, he probably did not go to a university, yet in one way or another he learned Latin, Portuguese, and Spanish. After being a common seaman, he moved up in society to become a tradesman, selling maps. Then he had the good fortune to marry a noblewoman, which made him more eligible to enter court circles. And like everyone else, Columbus was helped by the fact that, thanks to a German named Johannes Gutenberg, books were coming out in print. Gutenberg invented movable type in the 1440s, and by 1490 printing presses were in operation all over Europe. With so many different kinds of books suddenly available, change took hold in Europe.

The Adoration of the Magi (1504), by the German painter Albrecht Dürer. Although the subject is a standard biblical one, the landscape and the human figures are contemporary.

THE REBIRTH OF ITALY

The change in people's minds, however, first began in Italy. This new age, which would later be called the Renaissance (or "rebirth"), was a time when people seemed to wake up, look around, and decide that, in spite of worries, life could be *enjoyed*. An Italian poet, Petrarch, is said to be the first man who ever climbed a mountain just for fun. Up to this time mountains had been merely barriers, nothing to be admired, but now people were finding beauty in places they had never noticed before. Indeed they were looking at everything differently, most of all themselves. Although God ruled supreme, why should people feel insignificant? they asked. God made people, so people had the power to create, to remake the world, to become more than puny little no-account beings of flesh and bones.

It was the ancient Greek and Roman writers and artists (living as long ago as the fifth century B.C.) who inspired this new thinking. The Greeks and Romans had always been a part of history, but

BELOW LEFT: *A Roman statue, from the first century A.D., of the god Apollo. It was based on a Greek statue several hundred years older.*

BELOW RIGHT: *Sculpted in marble,* La Pietà, *by Michelangelo, is one of the wonders of the Italian Renaissance. Compare the flowing fabric and lifelike human figures to the ancient Roman statue.*

now they seemed to step out of the past and challenge a world dominated by religious concerns. Of course there was a Heaven and Hell, but what about the here and now? The ancient Greeks and Romans had celebrated life; their sculptors were not ashamed to portray human bodies in the nude, nor were their philosophers hesitant to speculate about what went on in the minds of men and women. So people began asking questions, studying, discovering, collecting ancient treasures. When architects built churches, they tended to abandon the Gothic style of soaring arches, which was popular in the eleventh and twelfth centuries. More churches were built with pillars and domes, where people felt uplifted but not lost in the space around them.

The new artists, however, were far too stimulated just to copy old forms. Freed by the classic masters, they observed life and created their own interpretations. Gradually the Renaissance spirit spread over Europe, but nowhere was it more intense, more electrifying, than it was at its height in the city of Florence, where it began.

BELOW LEFT: *View of the Gothic cathedral at Chartres, France. Vertical lines, elongated arches, and soaring spires pull the eye upward.*

BELOW RIGHT: *In contrast, the rounded domes, designed by Michelangelo, atop St. Peter's Cathedral in Rome contain the eye.*

THE GLORIES OF FLORENCE

Unlike some other areas of Europe, Italy was not a unified nation under a central government. Instead, it consisted of city-states— Rome, Milan, Venice, Genoa, Naples, and Florence were the most important—and perhaps for this very reason it was more receptive to new ideas. These city-states had prospered, were stimulated by rivalry, and because they were smaller units with local pride, they branched out into art. Florence, a city of marble statues and massive stone buildings, was not only the artistic center of Europe, it was the banking center. And it was the only city that managed to be a democracy even for short spurts. Still, even when they had a dictator, Florentines called him their "first citizen" and thought of themselves as democratic. Certainly they were politically minded and independent (they dressed not according to fashion, but as they pleased), and they were jealous of their rights to the point of belligerency.

At the same time they were so proud of being Florentine that, no matter how miserable conditions may have been for some, they shared, rich and poor, a sense of brotherhood. They agreed that Florentines were superior to other Italians. Still, each Florentine wanted to be the best. At one time a number of citizens were caught up in a competition to build the tallest tower. So up they went, these towers, higher and higher until Florence looked like a city on tiptoes straining into the sky, its towers two hundred feet and sometimes higher. Obviously this couldn't go on, so in 1250 a law was passed limiting towers to ninety-six feet. Temperamentally, the people of Florence were exactly the kind to grab on to new ideas and run with them. And temperamentally, Lorenzo de Medici was exactly the kind of man to lead Florence into its golden age.

LORENZO THE MAGNIFICENT

Twenty years old in 1469, when he came into power as Florence's first citizen, Lorenzo de Medici was a handsome, generous, high-spirited man who, like all Italian leaders of his day, enjoyed power, indulged in intrigue, and sallied forth to war from time to time. In 1480, when he emerged from a series of such conflicts, he was not

OPPOSITE: *This 1470 Italian miniature shows a crowded city street with vendors and merchants competing for business.*

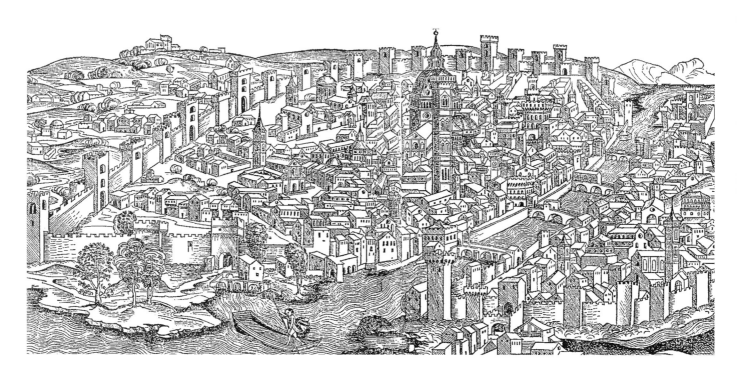

View of Florence, from a 1493 German woodcut.

only the foremost leader in Italy but was Florence's hero—Lorenzo the Magnificent. He had acquired rivals and enemies, as all heroes do, so whenever he went out, he was preceded by ten armed guards. One held aloft a drawn sword as a precaution. But Lorenzo was a man of the people, hard-working, joyous, impulsive, one who liked joking, dancing, singing, wrestling, playing tennis, collecting ancient gems for his private museum, buying Greek manuscripts for his library, adding statues to his grandfather's famous garden, and talking, talking, talking. His hero was the Greek philosopher Plato, and he met regularly with a small group who called themselves the Platonic Academy. When Lorenzo wrote a letter, he closed with "Yours in Plato." Whatever he did, he did with his whole heart. To celebrate the feast of St. John (Florence's patron saint), Lorenzo presided over sixty days of city revelry: parades, plays, feasting, pantomimes, music, poetry—some of which Lorenzo himself wrote. According to one Florentine, there were "so many fifes and music, songs, dances, and other festivities, and merrymaking, that this earth seems like a paradise."

Paradise would not have seemed out of reach to people in fifteenth-century Florence. Anything was possible for them. Art was no longer limited to a religious lesson or a commemoration of holy days or a celebration of military victories. Art was enjoyed for its own sake simply because it was beautiful, and no one was a more enthusiastic patron of the arts than Lorenzo de Medici. Once, so the story goes, he came upon a young man carving a statue of a faun, a Roman god who was half man, half goat. Lorenzo asked him what he was carving. "An old faun," the young man replied. Well, it didn't look old to him, Lorenzo commented; the teeth were too good. Immediately the sculptor knocked out one of the front teeth. Lorenzo was so amused, he invited the young man to move into his palace. The man was Michelangelo, and he stayed in the palace for four years.

The wonder of the Florentine artists, however, was that they were often not only artists but proficient in many other skills; the term *Renaissance man* today refers to a person who excels in a wide variety of activities. They were interested in everything and seemed able to do whatever they wanted. Leon Battista Alberti died a few years after Lorenzo came into power, but for generations people talked about his accomplishments and quoted his wise and witty sayings. Alberti was a landscape artist, an architect, a writer, a lawyer, a musician, a mathematician, and a spectacular gymnast who with his feet tied together could leap over a man's head. Or so people claimed.

LEONARDO

The most accomplished man of his time and perhaps of all times was Leonardo da Vinci. He was interested in *everything*, not only in what was already in the world but in the infinite possibilities of what he might put there. Unlike that other great artist of his day, Michelangelo, who was a loner, unkempt, and difficult to get along with, Leonardo was handsome and affable, and so afire with ideas that it was sometimes hard for him to stay with one project long enough to finish it. When he was working on his famous painting *The Adoration of the Magi,* he spent so long sketching alternative ideas that he became impatient with the final version and left the finishing to others. When he was painting *The Last Supper,* he walked the streets, looking for faces that were right for the disciples. When he found one, he rushed home to make a sketch. It took him three years to find and paint all the disciples, but when he was ready to paint Christ, he could find no one per-

fect enough. Indeed, he couldn't even imagine a face that would be right, so once again he abandoned the painting and had someone else add the head to his figure of Christ. Michelangelo, who was said to be jealous of Leonardo, accused him of never finishing anything. That was not quite true. Still, ideas crowded upon Leonardo so fast that he could hardly wait to start on the next one.

He wanted not only to paint; he wanted to invent. Once he wrote to the ruler of Milan, applying for a job as a military engineer. He would build bridges that were easy to carry, he said; make cannons that could hurl stones so thick and fast, they would seem like hail; design tunnels that would go under water; invent armored cars in which the drivers would be safe from enemy attack. Later he would dream up a contraption with bellows hidden inside for frightening the enemy's horses. He invented the parachute, drew plans for making a water mill that would play music while it turned, designed skis for walking on water, and, in the same year Columbus first sailed into the unknown, sketched his idea for a flying machine. Perhaps his most practical invention was an adjustable monkey wrench, and his most playful one was a mechanical lizard with beard, horns, and wings that fluttered when injected with mercury.

Leonardo was not satisfied simply to follow conventional ideas in art; he thought for himself, always observing nature. He studied anatomy at a hospital so that when he drew a human figure, he could visualize the bone structure beneath the clothes. In the past, artists had always painted halos above the heads of saints and holy figures. Not Leonardo. He had never seen a halo and he never painted one. As fascinated by science as he was by art, he studied rocks, stars, rivers, men, and women, always fighting to grasp the secrets behind what he saw. He suggested that the sun did not move around the earth, as people believed; the earth moved around the sun. He said that the Sahara Desert had not always been a desert; it was once covered by salt water. He died in 1519 at the age of sixty-seven, a man who embodied the Renaissance, which by then was changing all of Europe.

Although Leonardo was the most inventive man of his time, this period is known more for its art than its science or its inventions. Still, innovations were taking place. In 1489 the symbols + (plus) and − (minus) came into use, making life easier for school children as well as mathematicians. By the mid-1300s professional clock-

OPPOSITE: Portrait of Ginevra de'Benci, *by Leonardo da Vinci. With the new belief in the importance of the individual, people who could afford to do so had their features recorded for posterity.*

Clocks came into wide use in the fifteenth century, changing the way people thought about time. The famous Strasburg clock, which included an astrological calendar, began operating in 1571.

makers were traveling from city to city to make and erect huge clocks for the tops of public towers. The oldest surviving mechanical clock in the world is in Salisbury Cathedral, in England; built in 1380, it still rings. Eyeglasses may have been invented by chance, but they obviously helped Petrarch, poet and lover of mountains. "To my annoyance," he wrote sometime between 1364 and 1374, "I had to seek the help of eyeglasses." In 1500 black lead pencils appeared in England, and in 1503 pocket handkerchiefs were invented.

WHAT ABOUT MORALITY?

But change never proceeds in a straight line. While some people rushed ahead with new ideas, some were afraid and clung desperately to the old. Indeed, there were those who even disapproved of eyeglasses. God gave people eyes, they said, to see the truth; eyeglasses distorted it. Some were suspicious of printing. But it was the new free exercise of the mind that was most disturbing. All this talk of the here and now! some grumbled. It was as if God Himself was being questioned. What did *people* know? they asked. They should be glorifying God, not celebrating themselves. What had happened to morality?

Savonarola, a priest in Florence, was particularly outraged. He was a man who seemed to have been born pious, and he couldn't bear to be with people who were not as pious as he was. Yet he expected a great deal of himself, too. All men were worms, he said, and he beat himself for being just another worm. When he went to college, he was offended by the bad language he heard. He quit and entered a monastery, where he expected to find piety at last. He didn't. The church, he found, was corrupt too. Even the pope, Innocent VIII, led a worldly life, commissioning art from Florence, living in luxury, ignoring his vow of celibacy, fathering illegitimate children. Most shocking, perhaps, was the fact that the church sold pardons for sins, or indulgences—time off from Purgatory. It was as if it didn't matter how much wrong people did; they could still get to Heaven if they confessed and paid the church enough money.

Since Savonarola didn't feel at home anywhere in the world, it was obvious he would have to change the world, including the

Savonarola.

church. He became a preacher. At first he was unimpressive, but gradually he came to realize that he was not going to rouse his audience by using reason. He would have to get angry, to shock and frighten. So he let himself go. All the rage he had stored up inside he turned on his audience, lashing them as if he were using a whip. "Repent!" he screamed. "Repent!" People flocked to hear him. The more insulting he became, the more they loved it. "Ye women," he cried, "who glory in your ornaments, your hair, your hands, I tell you, you are all ugly." He preached against Florence—its naked statues, its proud rulers, its vain citizens. He railed against the clergy, even the pope. At Lent he sent boys from his church around the city, collecting what he called "vanities"—playing cards, wigs, cosmetics, dice, musical instruments, pictures, and books that he considered wicked. Then a huge bonfire was built and the vanities were thrown in and burned.

Even in his solitude he worked himself into such an emotional state that he went into trances, claiming to see into the future. In a sermon he predicted that Lorenzo and the pope would die in 1492. When they both did die in that year, people hailed

A 1489 map shows Europe's conception of the world just before Columbus's voyage. Australia and the Americas, of course, are missing entirely.

Savonarola as a prophet and came to hear him in even greater numbers. And now Savonarola was inspired to new heights of eloquence, for the new pope, Alexander VI, was even more corrupt, more worldly, more ambitious than the last one. Savonarola didn't just preach his anger, he performed it, hurling imaginary bolts of lightning into the audience, turning his voice into crashes of thunder, whispering ghostly messages of doom. What the pope objected to, however, were the prophecies, which Savonarola insisted came directly from God. This was heresy, and the pope invited Savonarola to Rome to talk. Savonarola would not go. Defying the pope at every turn, he became more and more intoxicated by his own power. "Bring in the excommunication," he cried; "bring it on a spear! I crave only the Cross; make me to be persecuted." He even wrote the rulers of European countries, begging them to call a meeting to reform the church. "I testify," he wrote, "that this Alexander is no pope."

Now he had really gone too far. His letter was intercepted, the

pope saw it, and Savonarola was put on trial for heresy. On May 23, 1498, he was hanged and burned. Although by this time his popularity had waned, there were still people who put flowers on the spot where he had died and others who continued to do so on the anniversary of his death for over two hundred years. Pope Alexander lived for five more years, but he was so corrupt and unpopular that when he died, people danced in the streets, and it was said they stuffed his body into a coffin that was too small for him.

THE KNOWN AND UNKNOWN WORLDS

In spite of Savonarola and others who held to a strict biblical approach to life, new ideas were taking hold. Although *geography* was a word that did not even enter the English language until the middle of the sixteenth century, people wondered about the world. What was its shape? And its size? For centuries the only world maps people saw were of the world as pictured in the Bible. At the center of the maps was Jerusalem; at the top, marked east, was the Garden of Eden. And since the Bible spoke of the "four corners of the earth," that meant the world was flat. But now people were reading ancient writers again. They were rediscovering Aristotle, a Greek who lived from 384 to 322 B.C. When Aristotle observed that the shadow of the earth on the moon during an eclipse was curved, he concluded that the earth must be a sphere. Then there was Claudius Ptolemy, an Egyptian who lived five hundred years after Aristotle and drew a map with eight thousand place-names on it and with north clearly at the top. Before long most educated people agreed that the earth was indeed a sphere, and most mapmakers were placing north at the top of their maps.

But their world was small. Though Europe might be out of shape in spots, at least it was all there. But not Africa. Only the top third of Africa appeared; the rest was either blank or simply imagined. The outline of Asia was vague, with the southern tip sometimes swinging around to join an imaginary extension of Africa. On a map like this, the Indian Ocean was an enclosed body of water. And the rest of the world? There was no rest. That was all there was, except for the vast Ocean Sea that surrounded the world but went nowhere.

But who could be sure what the world was like? Although some people insisted that what wasn't known could never be known, others were curious. Was there a way to reach Asia by water? they asked. What happened to the southern part of Africa? Could a ship sail around Africa and reach the spice markets directly? The first Europeans who tried to find out were the two Vivaldo brothers, from Columbus's home town, Genoa. They left Genoa in May 1291, and though it was known that they reached Cape Nun on the northwest coast of Africa, nothing more was ever heard of them.

Perhaps this discouraged other explorers, because it was not until 1419 that we learn of a Venetian merchant, Nicolo de Conti, setting out to find that spice market. His travels were by both land and sea, and he ranged from north Africa to Burma, and to the islands of Ceylon (with its cinnamon forests), Sumatra (with its pepper trees), and Java. He returned to Venice after twenty-five years with an Indian wife, four children, and the firm conviction that ships could sail around Africa and reach the spice markets of India.

HENRY THE NAVIGATOR

But someone still had to do it. Prince Henry of Portugal (1394–1460) had always been curious about the unknown world and was determined to make a systematic business of finding out about that mysterious African coastline. Once, when Prince Henry's brother invited him to go on a tour of Europe, he declined. He wasn't interested in the known world, he said; he wanted to discover the unknown one. So on the southern tip of Portugal he set up a naval headquarters, a school for seamen, and a center for gathering information. He consulted with physicists, astronomers, mathematicians, and he invited Master Jacome, a famous Jewish geographer from the island of Majorca, to be a kind of expert-in-residence. In addition, he built a new type of sailing ship, the caravel, which had three sails instead of two and was lighter to handle. He figured this would make it easier for his explorers to sail against the wind and come home. After all, it was no use for them to go out if they couldn't get back.

Each time he sent explorers down the coast of Africa, he told

Prince Henry the Navigator, of Portugal.

them to go as far as possible. When they came back too soon—and they usually did—Prince Henry was patient. "Go again," he would say. "Only this time go farther." Cape Bojador, a bulge in the coast south of Cape Nun, was what stopped the ships. It was not so much what the explorers saw that frightened them, but what they imagined was there. According to all the old stories, Cape Bojador was the beginning of the Green Sea of Darkness, an end-of-the-world area where the waters boiled, people turned black, and the air was poisoned.

"Don't believe all you hear," Prince Henry told his men, and he sent them right back.

In 1434 Gil Eanes, a young man brought up in the prince's household, did manage to round the cape and put to rest those stories. Gradually Prince Henry's explorers inched farther and farther down the coastline, bringing back gold dust, ivory, and the most profitable of all commodities—slaves. Prince Henry had the slaves baptized, which may have eased his conscience, but what was most important to him was finding out how that coastline ended.

Prince Henry never did find out. He died in 1460, and it was not until twenty-eight years later, in 1488, that Bartholomew Diaz, another Portuguese, rounded the tip of Africa and saw that the Indian Ocean was not enclosed after all. He could sail right across it to the rich markets of India, and he was ready to do that. But his crew wanted to go home. They threatened to mutiny if he didn't turn around. So he turned around. Although he wanted to return and do it right the next time, that job was given to Vasco da Gama, who reached Calicut in 1497.

CHRISTOPHER COLUMBUS

In 1492 Christopher Columbus set out for China on a shortcut—straight across the Ocean Sea. Going across the Ocean Sea was generally considered an outrageous idea. After all, no one knew what was out there; no one knew how wide that ocean was; no one could imagine sailing blindly into nowhere. The king of Portugal didn't believe such a journey was possible; neither did the king of England, and it took Christopher Columbus six years to talk Queen Isabella and King Ferdinand of Spain into supporting his

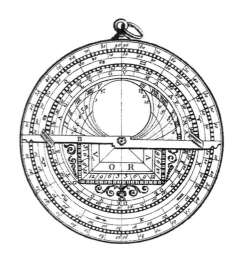

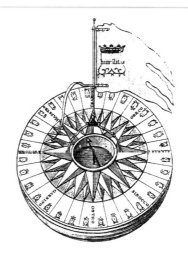

The invention of the mariner's compass enabled fifteenth-century Europeans to navigate at sea more accurately.

expedition. But Columbus had no doubts. In the first place, he *wanted* China and Japan to be a short distance from Europe. And Christopher Columbus always believed just what he wanted to believe. He had read Marco Polo's account of his overland trip to China two hundred years before and was particularly impressed by what he said about the riches of Japan. Marco Polo had never been to Japan, but that made no difference to Columbus. He believed Marco. He believed Aristotle, who said there was a "small sea" between Spain and the Indies. And he believed the famous Italian scholar Dr. Toscanelli, who estimated that it was just three thousand miles between the Canary Islands and Japan.

As for Queen Isabella, she was in desperate need of gold after her expensive war with the Moors, so she wanted to believe Columbus, who talked of bringing back so much gold that she would even be able to make a crusade to Jerusalem. So she gave him a chance.

Columbus could not be described as a modern man, even in the way that Prince Henry had been. Although he was the first to undertake such a daring expedition, Columbus still had a medieval outlook on the world. He persuaded himself that he had been appointed by God to find the Indies. And since God could not be wrong, Columbus never doubted that he had found the Indies, no matter that the evidence was against it. He decided that Cuba was a peninsula off the coast of China and he made all his crew sign an oath that Cuba was indeed part of the mainland of China. When, on his fourth and last trip, he landed on what we now know was South America, he admitted that it seemed like a continent. But how could it be? he asked. The only continent around was China (Cuba), which was to the north. So he decided this must be the Garden of Eden.

Columbus's situation was different from that of the explorers who went down the coast of Africa. Those Portuguese had some idea of what to expect. Their job was to improve their navigational skills enough to realize what they already imagined. There were no big surprises on the way. Columbus, on the other hand, had the skills, but his mind was not ready for what he found. Indeed, it was hard for Europeans to make room in their thinking for an entirely new continent, but by the time Columbus died in 1506, most educated Europeans had accepted the fact that Columbus had stumbled upon a new world. But Columbus didn't accept it. He still

Christopher Columbus dressed as a Renaissance gentleman, in a painting done after his death.

insisted that he'd been close to Japan. One more trip, he said, and he would have found it.

Columbus's voyages changed the shape and character of the world. Before long other Europeans were crossing the ocean, returning with treasures, exploring the globe, settling down in what they called the New World. They were discovering that the world had far more people than anyone had imagined. And the people were different—different from Europeans and different from one another. Yet these new experiences did not change the way Europeans saw themselves. They did not doubt that they were the most civilized people in the world, and they expected the rest of the world to recognize their superiority and behave accordingly.

ASIA IN 1492
Katherine Paterson

When Columbus set sail from Spain in search of the Orient,
he carried with him a letter addressed "To the Great Khan."

Silent but for the pounding of thousands upon thousands of hooves, nomad warriors thundered down the steppes of central Asia, changing the face of the world. These horsemen traveled twice as fast as any other army of the time. They never stopped riding. With his own remounts following him like obedient dogs, a warrior could switch horses as soon as the one he was riding grew weary. Each man carried dried milk and strips of beef in his saddlebag, and when those ran out, he would slit a vein in the leg of his horse and drink the blood.

The horses were as hardy as their masters. They ate only the sparse grass of the steppes, and when there was snow, they pawed the ground until they uncovered the dry grass beneath.

The nomads called themselves by the names of their tribes—Mongol, Tatar, Naiman, Merkit, Kerait. The thirteenth-century Europeans whose lands they overran called them Tartari, the "People from Hell." Christians and Muslims considered these Asian nomads savages, but actually they formed the most sophisticated army in the world. During World War II, both the Germans and the Americans adopted tactics learned from the Mongols.

GHENGIS KHAN

They became known as Mongols because an orphaned boy of that tribe defeated all the other tribes on the steppes of central Asia. He bound his former enemies into a powerful military force totally obedient to him. They called him their Grand Khan. The word *khan* meant "Lord of Lords," and to this title was added the name Ghengis, which meant "very mighty."

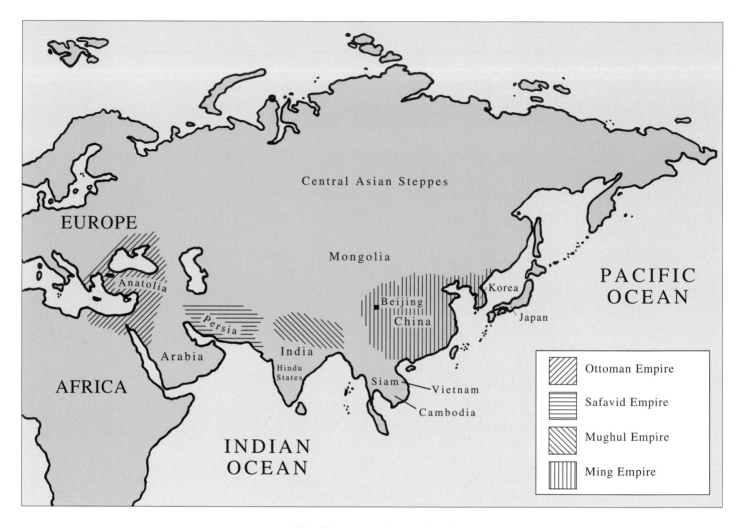

All of Asia and much of Asia Minor and Europe would feel the effects of Ghengis Khan's conquests for centuries to come. Certainly in 1492 the influence of the Mongols still was felt strongly in the varied kingdoms and empires of Asia. Most of Asia had been part of the Khan's empire, and even those nations that escaped actual conquest did not escape doing battle against him or his descendants.

Initially, Ghengis Khan led his mighty hordes off the steppes of the north and down into China, which had already been a great civilization for thousands of years. He conquered ninety cities, carrying off every thing and person of value to his army, including scholars and skilled workmen, and destroying the rest. He did this everywhere he went, always learning whatever he could from the nations he captured or wooed to his side.

With the brilliant strategy of Ghengis and his sons and generals, the Mongols swept through central Asia. Ghengis went on into Europe, and later his grandson and one of his generals went as far as Moscow, causing such devastation that for centuries one of the prayers recited daily in the churches of eastern Europe was, "From the fury of the Mongols, good Lord, deliver us."

Known as the Golden Horde, descendants of Ghengis ruled in eastern Europe for two hundred years, taking tribute from the Russians, until they were defeated by another descendant of Ghengis's hordes, Timur the Lame, better known in the West as Tamerlane. His conquests included not only Persia, Mesopotamia, and southern Russia, but northern India as well.

There was one European power that early recognized Ghengis Khan as no mere bandit. This was the merchant city of Venice. A secret pact was made between Venice and the Mongol Empire. Venetian merchants would gather information for the Khan in the countries they visited and spread what propaganda the Khan might desire those peoples to hear. In turn, the Mongols would destroy every rival trading station and leave Venice a trade monopoly in all the lands the Mongols conquered.

Ghengis himself died in 1227, but his empire did not die with him. He had made wise provisions. His last orders divided his vast empire among his surviving sons, selecting Ogedei to be Grand Khan in his place. His last words were about one of his grandsons. "Listen to the words of the boy Kublai, they are wise; he will one day sit on my throne and will bring you prosperity as I have done."

Ghengis Khan.

MARCO POLO

In 1275 two ragged merchants and a youth from Venice stood before the greatest ruler of the world. The journey across seas and mountains and deserts had taken over a year. Many years later, Marco Polo, who had been eighteen that day he first came to the court of Kublai Khan, wrote of the Mongol emperor: "In respect to number of subjects, extent of territory, and amount of revenue, he surpasses every sovereign that has heretofore been or that now is in the world; nor has any other been served with such implicit obedience by those whom he governs."

In the great city of Khanbalik (now called Beijing), which he had

The young Marco Polo. From an illustrated German edition of his memoir.

built, Kublai Khan lived in jeweled splendor surrounded by his nobles, who wore gold-embroidered uniforms. His empire stretched from Korea to the Arabian desert and eastern Poland. From as far away as Burma, people paid him tribute, and he was clever enough to pay his own debts not in precious metals but in flimsy printed paper, which quickly wore out. It could be replaced, but the owner was charged a fee to replace it.

In addition to the overland trade routes he maintained, Kublai Khan had ships that sailed the seas to trade and demand tribute. But he was not only a great administrator and a man of enormous wealth, he was a man of intellectual curiosity. He was fascinated by Chinese Confucian scholars, but he also assembled at his court in Khanbalik Buddhist and Muslim holy men and teachers. On their first trip to Cathay (or China, as we know it today) the Khan had asked the Polo brothers, Nicolo and Maffeo, to entreat the pope in Rome for one hundred Christian scholars who were not only well-versed in the Christian faith but in Western science, music, and the arts. But the pope supplied only two preaching friars, who lost courage and turned back for home long before the Polos crossed the Gobi Desert on their arduous and dangerous return trip.

The brothers had brought, however, Nicolo's teenage son, who quickly won the Great Khan's respect and affection. The young Marco Polo became a traveling envoy for the Khan and sailed as a ship's commander and ambassador to distant parts of the Khan's empire.

If there was a great, advanced civilization in China (as well as in many other parts of Asia and the Middle East) in the thirteenth century, why didn't other Europeans flock into Asia after the Polos' adventures were known?

Several things happened. Kublai Khan died in 1294, and before long a struggle for power within the vast Mongol Empire began.

Meantime, the great trading cities of Venice and Genoa were involved in a bloody struggle to control the Mediterranean trade. Marco Polo, because of his experiences as a commander of ships for Kublai Khan, was asked to take charge of a warship for the Venetian Doge. He was captured, and while in a Genoan prison he wrote a book telling of the wonders of Kublai Khan's empire and of his adventures in the Khan's service. Later the book was laboriously copied and distributed, for although the Chinese had begun printing books more than two hundred years before,

Europe would not "invent" printing for almost another two hundred years.

But Marco's book proved unbelievable to his eager readers. They could not imagine a king who observed the festivals of Christianity, Judaism, and Islam as well as those of his own native religions. They could not picture the luxurious court furnished with gold, silk, and precious jewels or the leopards that had been trained to hunt. They did not know kings whose every word was absolute law yet who took it upon themselves to feed and clothe the poor within their realm. The book was regarded by its readers as a fantasy. Marco protested to his deathbed that everything he had written was true, but it would be centuries before Europe would acknowledge the greatness of the ancient Asian civilizations.

A Mongol archer on horseback. From a fifteenth-century Chinese painting.

THE MIDDLE EAST

Meantime, on the Asian continent, great changes were taking place. In the part of Asia that we call Asia Minor, but which is more properly known as Anatolia, Osman I (ca. 1258–1326) had organized the Turks who lived in Anatolia into a powerful empire. The word Turk means "wanderer," for the chief population of Anatolia had descended, like the hordes of Ghengis Khan, from the nomads of north-central Asia. Ghengis's followers claimed that they were descended from a blue wolf. The Turks told of an ancestor who was a gray wolf. But Osman's followers did not like to be called Turks or to be reminded of their nomadic ancestry. They called themselves the Osmanis—the people of Osman. They became known in Europe as the Ottomans. The Ottomans succeeded for a time in driving the Mongols out of Anatolia. Their victory closed the trade route that the Polos had traveled and that Ghengis and his successors had maintained and policed.

The story is told that Osman became a convert to Islam after reading its holy book, the Koran, at the home of a pious Muslim friend. This he did in one night—though not in one sitting. The story says he stood up the whole time.

During the latter half of the fourteenth century, Timur the Lame, a descendant of one of the generals of Ghengis Khan, rose to power. With the same ruthlessness that had characterized the earlier Mongol conquests, he subdued the Ottoman Turks, devastated his own kinsmen of the Golden Horde in eastern Europe, and led his army into India. The city of Delhi did not recover for a hundred years.

Timur the Lame was a Muslim, and he was determined to take China and force the Chinese to accept Islam, but he died on the march eastward and the campaign was abandoned. After his death in 1405, Anatolia was for a while plunged into civil war, but the Ottoman Turks began to pull together, and soon they again controlled the area that we now call Turkey in their honor. Under Sultan Mehmet II, who came to power in 1451 at the age of nineteen, the Ottomans began to move toward the great city of Constantinople, just across the narrow Bosporus Strait, which divides Europe from Asia.

Constantinople was the capital of the Byzantine Empire, which was the remaining remnant of the eastern part of the ancient

OPPOSITE: *Ottoman painting from the fifteenth century. Because Muslims believe any depiction of Muhammad to be blasphemous, he is shown here covered by a veil.*

Roman Empire. It was founded by the Roman Emperor Constantine in A.D. 330, at which time he moved his capital from Rome. Constantine became a Christian convert and made Christianity the religion of the empire, but after his death, the empire was divided among his three sons. The western part disintegrated until it could no longer hold out against the Goths (a people from Scandinavia), who overran all of Italy in about A.D. 476. The Huns, who, like the later Mongols, were nomads from central Asia, overran much of eastern Europe at about the same time, but the Byzantine Empire, centered in Constantinople, remained the strongest power in Europe until about the middle of the eleventh century.

Constantinople was the capital of a Christian empire, but ironically it was captured by western crusaders in 1204. The crusaders' stated goal was to save Jerusalem from Muslim control, but they sacked Constantinople.

The crusaders weakened the Byzantine Empire, as did various bands of Turks, though art, religion, and learning continued to flourish, especially in Constantinople itself. When Mehmet II and his Ottoman army were about to take the city in 1453, Byzantine scholars, scientists, and artists fled to the West, helping spark the Renaissance in Europe. And since the Ottomans now firmly controlled all the land routes to east Asia, the capture of Constantinople also inspired Europeans to venture out on the ocean. With the fall of Constantinople, the Middle Ages, or Dark Ages, of Europe came to an end, and a new age of discovery and enlightenment began.

Since the days of the Crusades, Europeans have tended to fear the power of the Muslim Middle East. Because of this ancient prejudice, the gifts of that part of the world have often been neglected in Western accounts of history. If Africa saw the origins of humankind, Western civilization had its birth in the Middle East. Here agriculture began and most farm animals were first domesticated. Villages were established and the first cities were built. In the Middle East three of the world's great religions were born—Judaism and its offspring, Christianity and Islam. In the Middle East governments were first organized and the concept of law came into human thought. The Middle East saw the invention of writing and the first preservation of written records, or histories. Two thousand years before Christ, Babylonians had developed a geometry with which they could make precise astronomical mea-

surements. And the Arabs gave Europe a system of counting (we still call our numbers Arabic numerals) and the concept of zero, which makes mathematics as we know it possible. The Arabs also brought the decimal system from India to Europe in about A.D. 750, but the system did not come into general use until it was reinvented by a Belgian tradesman in 1585.

In European accounts, a great deal is made of the cruelty of the Ottoman Turks, but most of the armies of that day were cruel. Mehmet II, the conqueror of Constantinople, tried to be an enlightened ruler. He himself was a man of learning who spoke six languages fluently—Turkish, Greek, Arabic, Latin, Persian, and Hebrew. He knew Greek and Islamic literature and philosophy and a bit of science.

Mehmet II, in a portrait by the Italian master Bellini, who lived in Constantinople under the Sultan's patronage.

In the lands that he conquered, he allowed Christians and Jews to worship freely and to maintain their own cultures and customs within the Muslim empire. He was, in fact, so tolerant of the Greek Orthodox Church that a hope arose that the Sultan might convert to Christianity. This he never did, but his love for art prompted him to preserve the beautiful Christian mosaics that decorated the Cathedral of St. Sofia in Constantinople, even though the cathedral itself was turned into a mosque. Islam prohibits the representation of the human form, but Mehmet II ignored this rule in order to maintain the beauty of the building.

The tolerance that Mehmet II displayed was in stark contrast to the Christian attitude of that day and prompted the saying among many ordinary persons: "Better the turban of the Turk than the tiara of the pope."

Mehmet II also chose Christians to be in his government, and many Christians, whether to curry favor or because of genuine conviction, converted to Islam.

Mehmet's military conquests did not end at Constantinople. Turkish forces pushed farther and farther into Europe.

One of the Sultan's more infamous European foes was Vlad Dracul, the ruler of Wallachia, now part of Romania. Dracul was known for his extreme cruelty in an age when cruelty in war was taken for granted. In the Ottomans' campaign into Wallachia, the Sultan came upon a "forest of corpses"—twenty thousand rotting bodies of Bulgarian and Ottoman soldiers whom Dracul had ordered impaled on stakes and crucified. Dracul the monstrous ruler has lived on in legend as Dracula.

Mehmet II, now known as Mehmet the Conqueror, subdued nearly all of Anatolia and southeastern Europe. Now he landed on the heel of Italy and was headed for Rome. Only his death at the age of forty-nine in 1481 stopped his advance and kept Italy from Muslim rule.

His son Bayezid II, who ruled from 1481 to 1512, was not the empire builder that his father and later Ottoman sultans were. He was kept busy at home in Anatolia dealing with unhappy rival Muslim groups who were discontented with high taxes and what they felt was Mehmet's favoritism toward converts to Islam from Christianity. At the time of Columbus's voyage in 1492, the Ottomans were not the active military threat they had been a few years earlier.

CHINA

In China, the later Mongol emperors were far removed from the sturdy nomadic warriors of Ghengis's day. Although they admired alien cultures and used foreign advisers, they were suspicious of the native Chinese peoples. Government officials were cruel and corrupt. The chief adviser of the last Mongol emperor inspired many anti-Chinese laws. The native peoples could wear only certain colors, could not use certain words (such as those for long life and happiness), and were not allowed to speak or even learn the Mongol language. The adviser was not content simply to repress the Chinese. He suggested that everyone named Chang, Wang, Liu, Li, and Chao be executed. Since these are the most common of the one hundred Chinese surnames, he would have eliminated nine tenths of the population this way.

Meantime, terrible floods, droughts, and earthquakes devastated the land and reduced the peasants to starvation. To the Chinese, this was a sign that Heaven had withdrawn its favor from the dynasty of Ghengis Khan. The Chinese people rebelled against their Mongol rulers.

Among their leaders was a peasant Chinese soldier whom Ghengis himself might have admired. He united the scattered bands of peasant rebels into a fighting force and, after more than twelve years of war, drove the Mongols from power. In 1368 he was proclaimed the Emperor Hung Wu, founder of a new, native Chinese dynasty, called the Ming, which meant "bright" or "shining."

Hung Wu sought to be a different kind of leader from the Mongols. It is said that he told his generals: "When Kublai took a city, he destroyed all who were in it, but this is not my method. Do not slaughter recklessly. Do not burn the houses of the people. Do not even think of killing the Mongols unless they resist."

And as emperor he is said to have declared: "My wish is to bring back again the government of the Sages. Be loving and obedient to your father and your mother; respect your elders and your superiors; live in harmony with your neighbors; educate your children; do your work peacefully, and do no evil." These words echoed the teaching of Confucius, a Chinese philosopher who lived nearly five hundred years before Christ and who has had a powerful influence on Chinese thought ever since.

Hung Wu, the first Ming emperor.

Indeed, Hung Wu wished his nation to be fully Chinese. He banned Christianity and, in true Confucian style, reinstituted the examination system by which scholars of the empire were to be identified. From these scholars he chose government officials and his personal advisers.

In traditional Chinese thought, there were four classes of people: scholars, farmers, artisans, and merchants. Soldiers, however necessary they might be, were thought to be outside the proper order of society. Though Hung Wu himself had been an illiterate peasant who won the throne by force, he was determined to rule like a scholar king, not as a warrior in the mold of Ghengis and the other Mongol emperors.

Under the third Ming emperor, Hung Wu's son Yung Lo, the Chinese experienced their own age of discovery. The leader of the Chinese naval expeditions was a man named Cheng Ho. He was a Muslim eunuch whose father and grandfather had made pilgrimages to Mecca, but we know most about him from a tablet set up to honor a traditional Chinese goddess, the Celestial Spouse.

The stone tells of Cheng Ho's seven voyages, including trips to southeast Asia, Ceylon, several Indian ports, and ports along the Arabian peninsula and the African coast.

"We have," the tablet reads, "traversed more than one hundred thousand *li* of immense waterspaces and have beheld in the ocean huge waves like mountains rising sky-high, and we have set eyes on barbarian regions far away hidden in a blue transparency of light vapors, while our sails, loftily unfurled like clouds, day and night continued their course [rapid like that] of a star, traversing those savage waves as if we were treading a public thoroughfare. Truly this was due to the majesty and the good fortune of the Court and moreover we owe it to the protecting virtue of the Celestial Spouse."

In contrast to Columbus's three tiny ships with total crews of ninety men, Cheng Ho captained fleets of fifty-two to 317 ships, some more than four hundred feet long. Columbus's largest ship, the *Santa Maria,* was only 117 feet long.

The Ming emperor Yung Lo was a builder of cities as well as ships. Hung Wu had made Nanjing his capital, but Yung Lo moved the capital back to Kublai Khan's city of Beijing. If you go there today, your chief sightseeing trip will be to the Forbidden City within the city of Beijing, where Yung Lo built the magnifi-

OPPOSITE: The Ming emperor Yung Lo, in a painting done after his death.

Workers forge an iron anchor in this picture from the Ming period.

cent palaces and courtyards that were the seat of his government and the dwellings of the imperial household. At the southern end of the imperial complex lie the three-tiered marble Altar of Heaven and the round Temple of Heaven with its famous blue-tiled roofs, where the emperor went to pray on behalf of the people. Outside Beijing there still stand the tombs of the Ming emperors, one of which took six hundred thousand workers to build and rivals any tomb built for an Egyptian pharaoh.

The Ming dynasty fostered art of many kinds. New techniques of porcelain making and decorating were perfected. The exquisite blue and white porcelain that is known as Ming in the rest of the world was called "Mohammedan blue" by the Chinese, because they found that the cobalt blue the Persians used for their pottery could withstand the intense heat of Chinese porcelain furnaces.

Among Chinese painters, the Four Great Masters of Ming are remembered not only for their beautiful works of art but because these men served as examples of the true Chinese ideal of scholar-gentleman. These were great persons who loved the simple life and were devoted to their art. They refused the wealth and power that government position would have given them. They died as old men, poor but much honored and loved by their students and the common people.

Literature, especially drama and the novel, which had begun to prosper during the latter days of Mongol rule, flowered during the early years of Ming, but the greatest cultural achievement was the *Yung-lo tatien*—the great encyclopedia compiled between 1403 and 1408. Even for the Chinese, the project proved too enormous for printing. It contained 22,937 chapters in 11,095 volumes. More than two thousand scholars worked on the encyclopedia. Their aim was to gather and transcribe all aspects of knowledge that existed at the time.

These were not totally peaceful years. There were wars against Vietnam, and the empire had to contend with marauding Mongol tribes to the north and Japanese pirates along the coast. But in many ways the early years of the Ming dynasty were a golden age for China. Indeed, after the voyages of Cheng Ho, the Chinese concluded that there was no land in the world that rivaled their own in wealth and learning. They began to turn more and more inward, revering their own past and taking pride in their present achievements.

A fisherman pulls in his nets in this detail from a Ming ink painting done in a poetic, loose style.

Content in their land, which they believed to be the center of the earth (the very name of China in Chinese is the Middle Kingdom), the later Ming emperors began to cut themselves off from the rest of the world. The Great Wall was rebuilt in an effort to keep out enemies from the north. There were no more voyages of discovery like those of Cheng Ho. Indeed, the Ming began to pass laws against seafaring. Just when Europeans were setting out to conquer the oceans of the world, the Chinese, who had proven that they had the ships and the understanding of navigation to do so, put an end to voyaging for any reason.

When another Chinese eunuch in 1480 wanted to launch an expedition against Indochina, government officials ordered the records of Cheng Ho's voyages destroyed so that they could not be used for future voyages. By 1500 it had become a crime punishable by death just to build a junk (a kind of sailing ship) with more than two masts.

The Ming dynasty lasted for almost three hundred years, but its later years were not the bright and shining ones that Hung Wu envisioned. By 1644, China was overrun by the Manchus, who, like their Mongol neighbors, were nomads from the north.

JAPAN

When Ghengis Khan's grandson Kublai Khan was established as emperor of China and most of Asia that was not under his direct control paid him tribute as "Lord of Lords," the Mongols turned their attention eastward. There was Japan, a small island country in the China Sea. The Japanese not only did not pay tribute to the Great Khan, but they had ceased to trade with the Mongol Empire altogether.

The Japanese had decided that it caused much less strain on the national treasury to take the Chinese goods they wanted by piracy. The Mongols complained, and sometimes the Hojo Regent who governed Japan at that time made the pirates return their booty. But the situation was obviously a sore point for the Great Khan.

Kublai sent not one but six messages to the Hojo Regent at his capital in Kamakura. Kublai asked for formal trade to be reopened between the two nations and hinted broadly that when relations were not friendly, war often followed.

The Regent ignored the trade offer but took the hint seriously. The threat could not have come at a worse time. The country had still not recovered from a long period of civil wars between the Heike and Genji clans. There had been earthquakes, drought, and famine, which the people thought indicated divine disapproval, and on top of that there had been strange comets that seemed to foretell doom.

Nichiren, a Buddhist priest, walked the streets of Kamakura, calling the people to repent and return to the true faith of Buddha (which happened to be the brand he taught) or suffer destruction.

Ready or not, the Mongols came. The Japanese were a military people, long accustomed to fighting, but they were prepared only for a war of chivalry, wherein one samurai might challenge another on behalf of an entire army. The Mongols cared nothing for knightly honor. They fought in close-knit formation, slaughtering every living thing in their path. In place of the thundering horse hooves of the plains, they brought huge war drums, which they beat so loudly that the Japanese war horses were panicked.

The Mongols attacked several ports and would likely have conquered the nation had it not been for one thing. Japan was a group of islands, and the Mongols could get there only by sea.

The tiny Japanese fleet knew the waters of the Japan and China

OPPOSITE: *A Japanese samurai in full battle armor rides across this fifteenth-century painted screen.*

This imposing wooden sculpture guarded a Japanese temple.

seas and how to read the winds. They drove the Mongol fleet into a storm where many ships were lost and the rest limped off to Korea to lick their wounds and regroup.

The Japanese were better prepared for the second attack, but not nearly well enough. This time a fighting force of fifty thousand Mongols and Koreans was joined by one hundred thousand men from south China. It was the greatest naval flotilla the world had ever known.

A Mongol account of the outcome of this invasion can be read in *The Travels of Marco Polo.* In Japanese history, this event is

known as the *kamikaze* or "god wind," for a gale blew in from the north with such force that the enormous Mongol fleet was virtually destroyed.

The Japanese rejoiced, though the priests took all the credit. Hadn't their prayers saved the nation? The Mongols never returned, but the Japanese did not rest easy. For hundreds of years Japanese mothers could be heard to say to their crying babies: "Why are you afraid? Do you think the Mongols are coming?"

But the aborted Mongol invasion had devastating results nonetheless. Previous wars had been civil affairs, and the winning general could always reward his supporters by seizing his enemies' lands and distributing them to the faithful. After the Mongol war, there were no spoils to divide. The country had suffered great losses but had gained nothing that could be passed out to the winners. Moreover, the priests demanded payment for saving the nation through their prayers. The Hojo Regency began to crumble.

Out of the years of civil war that followed the Mongol threat, a new shogun (or military dictator) rose to power—Takauji, of the powerful Ashikaga family. Takauji moved his headquarters to the Muromachi section of Kyoto.

One of his first acts was to negotiate a trade agreement with the Ming emperor, Yung Lo. This proved a clever move on Takauji's part, as Chinese trade supplied the wealth that kept Ashikaga shoguns in power for the next two hundred years.

The Muromachi Period was never a totally peaceful one, but it was nevertheless a rich time for Japanese art. Ashikaga shoguns commissioned two of the loveliest buildings and gardens in Kyoto—the Kinkakuji (Gold Pavilion) and Ginkakuji (Silver Pavilion).

There is in the garden of the Silver Pavilion a tiny teahouse. The door of the teahouse is so low and narrow that in order to enter, a samurai had to remove both of his swords and crawl in on his hands and knees. Here in this humble setting, the great men of the Ashikaga shogunate would kneel and seek inner peace and esthetic nourishment through the Zen Buddhist ritual of *chanoyu*—the tea ceremony.

Most of the arts of the Muromachi Period were influenced by Zen Buddhism, with its emphasis on silence, simplicity, austerity, and intimacy with nature.

The Noh (meaning "skill" or "ability") drama, a very subdued combination of dance, music, and poetry, developed during this time. The masks worn by the actors are works of art as well. They are good examples of the sculptural heritage of Muromachi, for most of them are hauntingly tragic, reflecting the Buddhist view of the sadness and brevity of human life.

Painting during this period is as subtle as it is exquisite, emphasizing the smallness of humankind in the vastness of nature, and employing empty space as a vital element of the work. This again shows the influence of Buddhist thinking, for in the words of one Chinese poet:

> We turn clay to make a vessel:
> But it is in the space where there is nothing
>   that the usefulness of the vessel depends . . .

Even today, to understand Japanese art, you must always consider what the artist has *not* put into his work as important as what he has chosen to include.

The art of Muromachi, including the ritual of the tea ceremony, represents a particular element of Japanese sensibility, which the Japanese themselves call *shibui*. It is the same word used to describe the taste of a fruit (particularly a persimmon) that is not quite ripe and that puckers your mouth when you bite into it.

Shibui in art describes a quiet, very subtle, almost severe quality. Other periods in Japanese art exploded with noise and color, as can be seen in Kabuki theater and the vibrant paintings of the later Momoyama Period (1573–1615), but Muromachi art will be remembered and honored for *shibui,* still thought of by most Japanese as the most elegant expression of the Japanese spirit.

The greatest Japanese master of *sumi-e,* or ink-painting, lived from 1420 to 1506. He was a monk named Sesshu, whose fame was such that he was even asked to decorate a room in the palace in Beijing for the Chinese emperor. Sesshu's style is sometimes almost abstract, though his subject is nature and the insignificance of humanity before its grandeur.

"Truly," said a monk-poet of the period, "the beauty of life is its uncertainty." The Muromachi was certainly an uncertain period in the history of Japan, but not all of that uncertainty was lovely. The Ashikaga shogunate began to crumble during the terrible Onin

civil war (1467–77) and was destroyed by peasant uprisings and the revolts of Buddhist monks of the Ikko ("single-minded") sect in 1488.

Thus, just as Europe was entering a great period of progress and discovery, Japan was plunging tragically into what became known as the Sengoku Jidai—the Period of the Country at War.

KOREA

Forming a geographical bridge between China and Japan, Korea throughout its history has been affected for better or for worse by these two nations. Korean legend tells that the son of the Creator came to earth and fell in love with a beautiful young woman who had just been transformed from a bear. The Creator's son breathed on the woman, and she gave birth to Tangun, Korea's first king.

Korea was originally populated by nomads from northern Asia who brought with them legends and language that bear a kinship to those of the Mongols. We can't be sure when these migrations occurred, but we do know that by the seventh century A.D. several ancient kingdoms of Korea were united by the Silla king. Since that time Korea has remained essentially the same in population, language, and geographic boundaries.

Silla Korea was officially Buddhist in religion, but for its political structure it adopted the Confucian model from China. There was one significant difference, however. In Korea there was a powerful aristocracy, and these families were not interested in importing elements of Confucian thought that might threaten their power. The examination system for recruiting government officials was adopted, for example, but only boys from aristocratic families were allowed to take the examinations.

The last years of the Silla dynasty were marked by power struggles among these families and by rebellions from the oppressed lower classes. Trade was the only route to power and wealth open to the masses, and some of the merchants who traded with China and Japan began to act like little princes. One of the most powerful of them even dared try to contract a marriage between his daughter and the Silla king. He was assassinated for his impudence.

In 901 an insane monk who was the illegitimate son of the king

gathered supporters and declared himself a king in north-central Korea. Before long he was overthrown by one of his own followers, a man named Wang Kon, who eventually became the first king of the Koryo dynasty. The name Korea comes from this time.

In 1231, the Mongol hordes crossed the Yalu River into the Koryo Kingdom. The Koryo court holed itself up on an island and prayed for deliverance. Artists carved woodblocks of the Buddhist scriptures in one last effort to persuade Heaven to save Koryo. By 1258, however, the Korean military dictator was assassinated and the whole country fell to the Mongols.

Although in history books the Koryo dynasty is reported to have continued until 1392, after the Mongol invasion there was so much intermarriage between the Koryo kings and Mongol princesses that the royal line was as truly Mongol as it was Korean. When Kublai Khan attacked Japan, his ships sailed from Korea, which provided nine hundred vessels, a majority of the provisions, and several thousand men.

Once Hung Wu broke the back of Mongol rule in China, Korea found itself divided. Some of the leaders still supported the Mongols, others felt the time had come to make an alliance with the Ming emperor. The pro-Mongol faction prevailed and sent their leading general, Yi Songye, to support the Mongol cause. But on the way north, Yi changed his mind. He turned back, seized the capital, and became the first king of the Yi dynasty, which lasted more than five hundred years.

Yi immediately made peace with the Ming, paying the necessary tribute, and renamed his country with the ancient name Choson (or Chosen).

Buddhism had flourished under the Silla and the Koryo kings. Yi was determined to keep it in check. He seized the great landholdings of the monasteries and gave the land to his supporters. The land immediately adjacent to the new capital (the word Seoul means "capital") was given to his closest associates and advisers. He rewarded his military leaders with landholdings farther out, where they would be handily located in case the Chinese, the Mongols, or the Japanese decided to attack his kingdom.

This divided the landholding class into two parts: the civil authority, located in and around Seoul, and the military authority, in the outlying areas. The landholding class was known as the *yangban*, which meant literally "two groups." Yi revived the Chi-

OPPOSITE: *This fourteenth-century Korean hanging scroll depicts the Buddha in a typically serene and balanced attitude.*

nese system of examinations, which had fallen into disuse during the later years of the Koryo, but only sons of the *yangban* were allowed to take the examinations.

Although life was hard for the lower classes and slaves, culturally the early years of Yi remain a shining period in the history of Korea.

Although the Korean language, like the Japanese, is more closely related to the languages of the nomads of northern Asia than it is to Chinese, for many centuries Chinese persisted as the only written language in Korea. All the examinations were in Chinese and were based on the Chinese classics, so the *yangban* were quite comfortable reading and writing Chinese. In fifteenth-century Korea, a wealth of scholarship was produced—encyclopedias, geography books, books on Confucian philosophy and learning, law books, histories—all, of course, written in Chinese but printed on movable-type presses perfected in Korea.

Koreans also produced astronomical instruments and a rain gauge, but the greatest invention of the time was a written language. Some scholars say that in its purest form, the phonetic Korean language, called *hang gul,* is the most logical system of writing in use anywhere in the world. Of course, the *yangban* scholars largely ignored the new Korean written language, but it came to be used in scientific works, by the lower classes, and by women. Since the symbols of *hang gul* were phonetic, corresponding to the sounds of the Korean language, it was far easier to master than the intricate characters of Chinese writing.

Korean pottery had long been admired by both the Chinese and the Japanese. The pottery of the Yi period was not as elegant as that of earlier years. Like the *hang gul,* it was more the craft of the lower classes, less refined but more practical and original.

Following a Confucian model, the Yi government had—in addition to the various departments for war, justice, revenue, and so forth—several boards whose sole purpose was to criticize the king and other government officials. As the emperor of China was usually a revered and distant figure, the criticism boards in China never amounted to very much. In Korea, however, it was a different story. Everybody in government was born into an aristocratic family, and consequently no one was particularly awed by anyone else.

The Boards of Censors could have been a helpful democratic

corrective, but in fact they became very divisive. Toward the end of the fifteenth century, a group of younger men in the *yangban* felt the censors should have an even greater role in guiding government policy. This made the older officials nervous, and they in turn tried to limit the function of the censors.

It happened that the king of the time (Songjong, 1469–94) had come to the throne as a young boy. He had been raised by the court advisers in the Confucian ideals, so he thought it was his duty to listen carefully to his advisers. The younger advisers were all for this. They proceeded to be so critical of every act of every official that it became almost impossible for the government to function at all.

Yonsan, the next king, put up with this state of affairs at first, but he gradually turned against those who supported a strong role for the censors. The fifteenth century, which had begun as a golden age, ended in bloody purges as Yonsan sought to execute or banish any official he thought was expressing, or had ever expressed, presumptuous opinions during his own or his father's reign.

SOUTHEAST ASIA

The story of Vietnam, like those of Japan and Korea, is closely bound to the story of China. Like their more powerful neighbors, the Vietnamese too adopted Buddhist and Confucian ideas of government and morals. Initially, as well, the Vietnamese did not attempt to transcribe their own language, but used Chinese characters.

For long periods of its history, Vietnam was a Chinese colony, but not happily so. The Ming emperor may have meant to be a more merciful conqueror than Ghengis Khan, but in truth the Ming conquest of Vietnam was cruelly repressive.

As one Vietnamese writer said: "Were the water of the Eastern Sea to be exhausted, the stain of their [the Chinese] ignominy could not be washed away; all the bamboo of the Southern Mountains would not suffice to provide the paper for recording all their crimes."

Ironically, Vietnam had largely escaped the devastation the Mongols had wreaked elsewhere. The secret of their successful guerrilla warfare was a unified, determined people. The king asked

A fifteenth-century Vietnamese porcelain jug in the shape of a duck.

the general who had saved Vietnam from the Mongols what he should do if the hordes should threaten the kingdom again. The dying hero answered: "The army must have one soul like the father and son in the family. It is vital to treat the people with humanity, to achieve deep roots and a lasting base."

The country was not of one soul when the Ming threatened. Many of the scholars and officials, who had trained in Confucian thought, actively collaborated with the invaders. But a patriot named Le Loi, following the tactics and advice of the hero general of the Mongol wars, gathered support and, after nine years of guerrilla warfare, regained Vietnam's independence.

Le Loi was loved by the people because during all those years he never allowed his troops to pillage or in any way to harm civilians. He was not so merciful with those who had collaborated with the enemy. He had them all executed.

In some ways Le Loi was a great reformer. He redistributed the land so that no one person could have control over a vast area and no land would lie uncultivated. Vietnamese replaced Chinese as the language of scholars as well as the speech of common people. Literature began to be written in Vietnamese.

It promised to be a wonderful time for the nation, but Le Loi brutally put down rebellions against his regime. Though Le Loi died of natural causes only six years after he became king, his son, who succeeded him, died mysteriously, and Le Loi's closest friend and most brilliant general was executed. The Le dynasty lasted about a hundred years, but Le Loi was almost the only king of his line to die of natural causes. The heroic and benevolent spirit that vanquished first the Mongols and then the Chinese disappeared into bloody struggles for power.

The other countries of south Asia (Thailand, Burma, Laos, and Cambodia) to which we give the broad title Indochina were really far more influenced by India than they were by China. A look at the map may suggest why. With the exception of inland Laos, these countries face India across the Bay of Bengal.

While Rome was still the great power of Europe, India was trading with Indochina, riding the monsoon winds that blow from India toward Indochina from late May to early October, and the opposite direction from November to May. With trade came significant elements of Indian culture—Buddhism (of a different sect from that which took root further east), elements of Hinduism,

varied art forms, crafts, and literature, especially Sanskrit poetry.

The influence of Indian architecture can be seen, for example, in Angkor Wat, a temple to Vishnu (a Hindu deity) that stands in Cambodia. The temple was built during the wealthy Khmer Kingdom of the twelfth century. Khmer builders and craftsmen certainly learned from their Indian counterparts, but their works in stone and bronze are unique.

During the fifteenth century the real power in Indochina was Siam (today's Thailand). Although Siamese kings accepted Chinese sovereignty in name, they were a long way from Beijing. They

The great Hindu wat, *or temple, at Angkor, Cambodia.*

strengthened their own power, borrowing from other nations whatever might help: from the Khmer they took a system of writing and model of government, from the Mongols they learned military organization. They adopted Theravada Buddhism, which originated in India, as their state religion.

INDIA

India, whose beginnings as a civilization are lost in the mists of prehistory, was not just a goal of Columbus's aborted voyage. It was and continued to be a much coveted jewel of many a conqueror's crown, from Alexander the Great in the fourth century B.C. to the British empire-builders of more modern times. But India is a vast and diverse subcontinent, difficult to conquer and almost impossible to rule.

In its long history India has given untold riches to the rest of the world. Both Hinduism and Buddhism began there, and Islam grew and developed in India. Christianity has existed there since the very earliest years of the Christian era. Perhaps only India could produce a twentieth-century saint like Mohandas Gandhi.

Of all India's religions, the most important is Hinduism. It came into the subcontinent with the Aryan peoples, nomads who moved down into India from lands near the Caspian Sea about 1500 B.C. These were people who loved the earth, the sky, the water, and who out of this reverence conceived of One who was beyond all beings. As an ancient poet expressed it:

> In the beginning there was neither naught nor aught:
> Then there was neither sky nor atmosphere above . . .
> Then was there neither day, nor night, nor light,
> nor darkness,
> Only the Existent One breathed calmly, self-contained.

This is the central idea of Hinduism—Brahman, the Existent One, the God above all gods, is the source of all life. Under Brahman there are many lesser gods, but all of them are simply different faces of Brahman. "Truth is One," the scriptures of Hinduism, the Vedas, declare. "They call him by different names."

Just as Jesus was Jewish, Buddha (ca. 563–483 B.C.) was

Hindu. He did not intend to start a new religion, but a new way of life. He saw about him great suffering, and it drove him to seek the cause of suffering and the meaning of life. Although he rejected the Hindu caste system, he did not deny the Hindu belief in reincarnation. This is the belief that when a person dies he or she will be born again on earth in another body—which may be human or animal, depending on the person's behavior in his or her previous life.

But Siddhartha Gautama, whom we now call Buddha (the name means "awakened," or Enlightened One), asked himself how a person might escape this cycle of many lives of suffering and sorrow and attain Nirvana—a oneness with the Oneness of Brahman.

After his enlightenment, he told his five disciples: "This is the Noble Truth concerning sorrow. Birth is sorrow, age is sorrow . . . death is sorrow." In other words, all of life was suffering

A page from a sixteenth-century Indian edition of the Bhagavata Purana, *a Hindu sacred book.*

and sorrow. The second Noble Truth, he said, was that sorrow comes from human desire, and will end only when humans cease to desire. The third Noble Truth was that persons can end desire by an eightfold path, which included: Right Views, Right Resolve, Right Speech, Right Conduct, Right Livelihood, Right Effort, Right Mindfulness, and Right Concentration.

The shared Hindu and Buddhist belief in reincarnation puts these religions in contrast to Islam and Christianity, which have their roots in Judaism. Judaism, Islam, and Christianity do not teach that human destiny is like a great wheel of birth and death and rebirth, but that each creature has only one life on this earth.

India gave the world more than two great religions. Sanskrit, the language of the Vedas, was the language of epic poetry and philosophy, as well as religion. India has produced great works of art and architecture, much of it inspired by religious beliefs and mythology. Medieval Indian science, especially medicine and surgery, was far in advance of the European science of the same period. The game of chess was invented in India. More importantly, so was the decimal system.

As for agriculture, Indians first domesticated chickens, rice, sugarcane, and cotton.

The spices, silks, and crafts of India were long in great demand in both Europe and the rest of Asia. Indian goods were often obtained through trade, but of course, powerful and greedy persons and nations sought to take the riches of India by force—though Ghengis Khan came into India almost by accident.

He pursued a wily Turkish prince named Jellal ad Din, one of the few commanders ever to defeat the Mongols in battle, into northern India. Ghengis sent part of his army up a cliff face so steep that a number of the horsemen lost their footing and plunged to their deaths. But enough survived to surround the Turks. Ghengis defeated Jellal ad Din's forces, but the prince himself managed somehow to escape across a fast-moving river. The Khan refused to let his men leap into the water to give chase. "Fortunate is the father of such a son," he said as he watched his enemy climb out on the opposite bank and make for safety.

The pursuit of Jellal ad Din proved to be the old Khan's last campaign. Carrying with them the spoils of northern India, the Mongols began to make their way homeward. The Slave dynasty of India (1206–90), so called because the founder had in fact been a

OPPOSITE: A page from the Shah-nama *(*Book of Kings*), a collection of adventure tales. Here, the demon Akvan throws the hero Rustam into the sea. This edition of the* Shah-nama *was produced in the first half of the fourteenth century.*

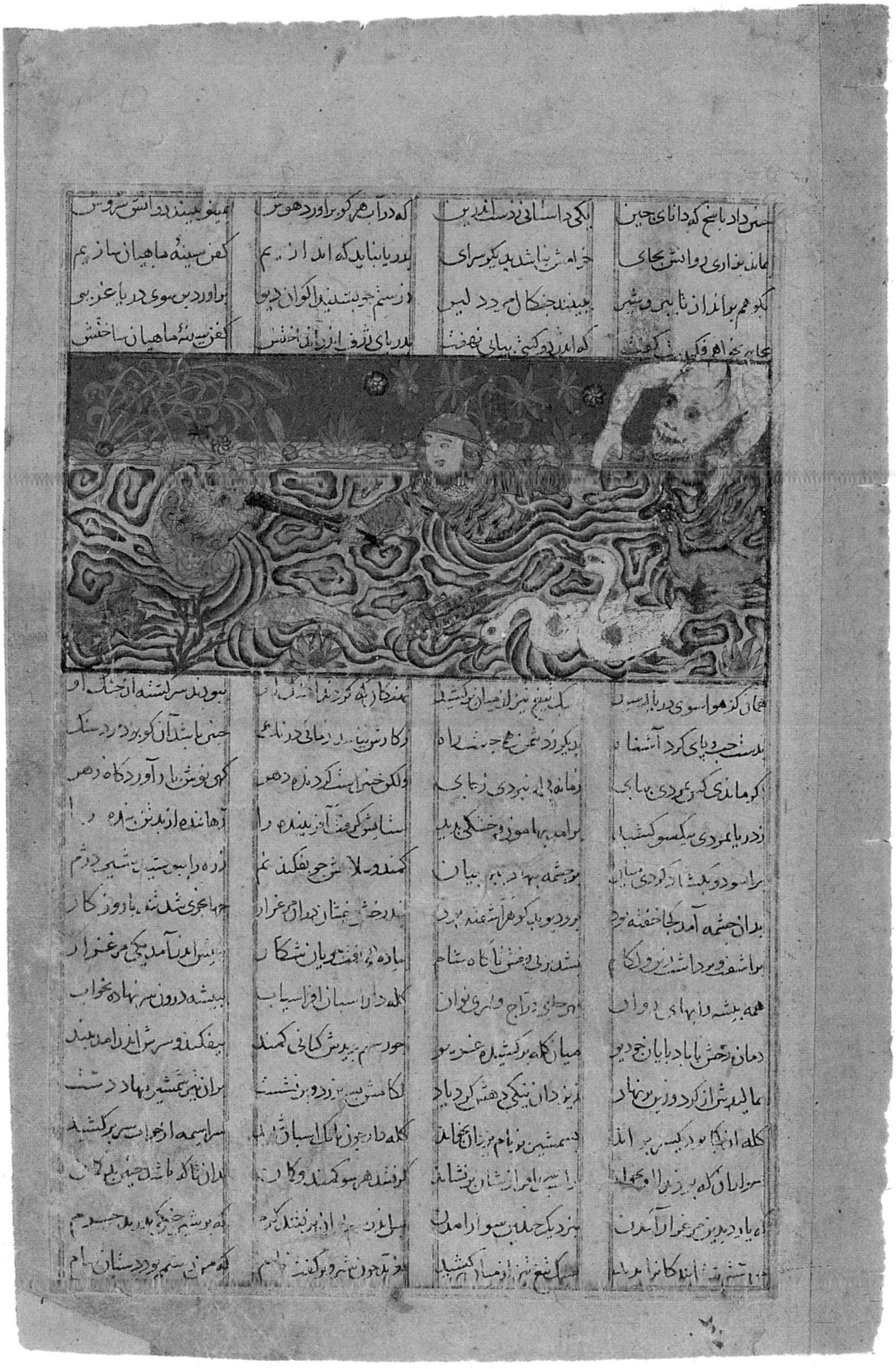

A twelfth- or thirteenth-century brass bodhisattva, *a Buddhist figure representing wisdom. From northern India.*

slave, was too weakened after the Mongol invasion to maintain control of the capital in Delhi. It was succeeded by the Khiljis, who themselves lasted only about thirty years.

During this period Mongol inhabitants who had converted to Islam attacked Delhi. The rebellion was brutally put down. The Khiljis sultan had the Mongol leader blinded. Mongol children were massacred and women given to the street sweepers of Delhi. Any men who survived the attack were trampled by elephants.

The general who put down the rebellion became the next sultan, Tughlaq I, the first of the dynasty by that name, which lasted until the beginning of the fifteenth century.

Meantime, the Mongol pacification of Asia Minor meant that India was not troubled by raids by the northern Turks or Afghans who had harried the country during the reigns of the Slave kings—although life under the first two Tughlaqs wasn't much happier as a result. Tughlaq I's son, Muhammad bin Tughlaq, was described by a contemporary as "a man who above all others is fond of making presents and shedding blood."

Perhaps his most infamous present was a cleverly constructed pavilion built for his father, who was still fighting battles even after he became sultan. Tughlaq I came home victorious, riding his war elephant. As soon as the elephant stepped onto the pavilion, the whole building came toppling in on elephant, rider, and all, leaving Muhammad a happy orphan and the new sultan.

Muhammad's son Firoz Shah Tughlaq was a great builder as well. But he was not the bloodthirsty man his father was, and his legacy included towns, hospitals, reservoirs, dams, mosques, colleges, bridges, and even public baths. But Firoz Shah did not attempt to unite the entire subcontinent.

For a long time India had existed as numerous separate states, some Muslim and the others Hindu. Thus in 1398, when Timur the Lame came fresh from his triumphs in Asia Minor and eastern Europe to add India to his conquests, there was no united force to meet him.

Timur was a Muslim who did not hesitate to slaughter Hindu "infidels," but most of the Indian Muslims of the ruling class belonged to the Sunni sect. Timur was a Shia Muslim. He spared Muslim theologians and those who could claim a direct kinship to the Prophet; the rest he made slaves. He also made slaves of "all the artisans and clever mechanics who were masters of their trades"

(his own words) and shipped them off to his capital, Samarkand, in central Asia. Timur's magnificent tomb, which still stands in Samarkand, is a monument to the work of the Indian craftsmen-slaves he deported there.

After Timur devastated much of northern India, he left it in search of other conquests. The last Tughlaq, who had fled before the defeat, returned to a devastated Delhi and a ruined kingdom. The next dynasty, the Sayyids (1414–51), were Mongol puppets, and they were succeeded by the Lodi kings, who were Afghan military rulers. The Lodi moved the capital from Delhi to Agra, but they became victims of their own squabbling nobles.

In 1498 the Portuguese explorer Vasco da Gama completed Columbus's aborted voyage to the Indies. Da Gama landed in Calicut in the southern Hindu kingdom of Vijayanagar. The West—first the Portuguese, followed by the Dutch, the Spanish, the English, the French, the Germans, and even the upstart Americans—would come often to the ancient and great nations of Asia, but they did not come as Marco Polo had, in wonder and humility. For the next five hundred years they would come as conquerors and plunderers, too often seeking to destroy that which they did not understand.

AFRICA IN 1492
Patricia and Fredrick McKissack

Africa is big. It's the second largest of the seven continents, with 11.5 million square miles of dancing grasslands, mysterious mountains, devouring forests, lazy rivers, watchful coastlines, and angry deserts.

Africa is old, too—probably the birthplace of humankind. The bones of the earliest direct ancestor of humans, a female nicknamed Lucy, were discovered in Ethiopia in 1974. This *Australopithecus* lived five million years ago.

Africa is a continent of extremes—sometimes lovely and serene, other times grotesque and full of rage, many times both at once. After all, Africa is home to some of nature's most unusual creations—hippopotamus, elephant, zebra, giraffe, crocodile, cobra, falcon, leopard, and lion—but not the Asiatic tiger! Africa is also the breeding place of the malaria-carrying *Anopheles* mosquito; the tsetse fly, which infects its victims with the deadly "sleeping disease"; and the insatiable ten-year locust.

Understanding Africa's massive and diverse land is the first step in trying to comprehend the peoples who carved out civilizations within its geographical extremes.

For example, in central Africa, at the edge of a vast rain forest covering a million square miles, men and women learned how to take metals out of the earth and craft them into tools and weapons. These they used to become more efficient masters of their environment.

In the soil-rich savanna-lands and plains of the Sudan, people planted seeds and harvested crops. They tended herds, hunted game, and built houses for their families.

Along the banks of four great African rivers—the Nile, the Zambezi, the Zaire (Congo), and the Niger—people made products for themselves and traded their surplus to others. They conquered their fear of the unknown and traveled from one side of the continent to the other, establishing trade routes and cultural exchange. As these commercial centers developed, so did the arts—painting, architecture, sculpture, literature, music, and dance.

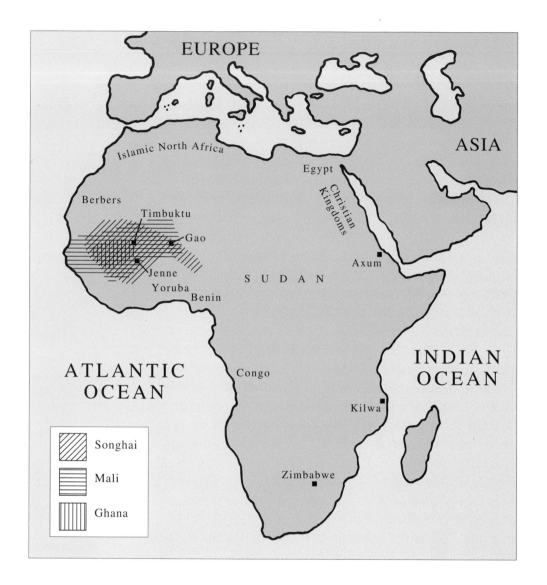

Fishermen made boats, mended their nets, and told stories on the peaceful banks of Lake Chad, Lake Victoria, and Lake Tanganyika. Their cousins living along Africa's great coasts wondered about the sea and what lay beyond. So they built ships and went exploring.

No doubt, at the foot of the great Ruwenzori Mountain Range—which soars 16,500 feet into the air, shrouded in clouds and covered with snow and ice year-round—men and women worshiped a power greater than themselves. From their gods they learned how to make laws and govern themselves accordingly.

Of course, all these things didn't happen at once. It took time—

millions of years. But slowly and steadily, Africa gave birth to numerous societies with distinctive customs, languages, and beliefs, many lasting to this day.

Africans were a major influence in the development of civilization. Egypt dates back to 8000 B.C. and was one of the earliest and greatest cultures of the ancient world. But Egypt wasn't the only great ancient civilization to spring up along the Nile. Egypt had well-established trade systems and diplomatic relations with the Nubian kingdoms of Kush, Alodia, Makuria, Meroe, and other sub-Saharan people of the Sudan. (At that time the Sudan—not to be confused with the modern-day nation of Sudan—was defined as the band of fertile grasslands just below the Sahara that stretched from the Atlantic Ocean to the Nile River.)

In ancient times, travelers from Asia and Europe explored the black kingdoms of the Sudan. Africans also visited the capitals of Europe and Asia. Trade and cultural exchanges between the three continents remained vigorous for centuries. Then there were times when powerful armies from the east and north claimed victories on African soil. And, in turn, African cultures triumphed over others.

ISLAMIC AFRICA

In Europe, during the year of Columbus's first voyage, Queen Isabella and King Ferdinand of Spain issued the Edict of Expulsion. The Islamic Moors of north Africa were Spain's primary target. Under the edict Jews and others who refused to convert to Christianity were exiled or burned at the stake. The Moors had ruled much of Spain since the eighth century, but in 1492 the Moorish King Abu Abdallah (Boabdil) surrendered Granada, their last stronghold in Spain. Although the Moors stayed on for almost a century, by 1610, through expulsion and migration, a million people, including many Jews, had retreated to northwestern Africa.

The Moors had conquered Spain as part of the Islamic *jihads* ("holy wars"), as prescribed by the teachings of Muhammad the Prophet.

Muhammad, an Arabian, was born in about A.D. 571. Muslims believe that when he was about thirty years old, the archangel Gabriel visited him and addressed him as "the prophet of God." It

Africans work the sails on this ship crossing the Persian Gulf. From a thirteenth-century edition of a book by the Arab scholar al-Hariri.

is said that Gabriel dictated Muhammad the Koran page by page.

Islam spread quickly, mostly because Muhammad's teachings spoke to the needs of different people—the rich, poor, young, and old. "All men are to be equal before their Maker," said Muhammad.

He also said, "I, the last of the prophets, am sent with the sword. . . . Slay all who refuse obedience to the law. Whoever fights for the true faith, whether he fall or conquer, will assuredly receive a glorious reward."

So during the eighth century, Arabs exploded across north Africa with the message of Islam: *There is no god but Allah, and Muhammad is his prophet.* The Muslims believed the spread of Islam was undertaken "for Allah's sake," the same way the Crusades were launched in 1095 by Christians "for the glory of God" and "the protection of His church."

Six years after Muhammad's death, Islamic armies had already conquered Arabia and much of Mesopotamia. Soon Persia, western India, and parts of China were a part of the Muslim empire, as were north Africa and most of Spain.

CHRISTIAN AFRICA

Three Christian African kingdoms struggled to survive the advancing Islamic armies: Egypt, Nubia, and Ethiopia. The Arab general Amru the Conqueror marched into Egypt in 640. By 642 Egypt was another pearl in the crown of Islam. Except for the Coptic Christian Church, which was allowed to continue at Alexandria, Christianity was all but wiped out.

Nubia, formerly a part of the ancient Kushite Kingdom, had been Christian since the sixth century. Nubia and Egypt had been trading partners since before the birth of Christ, sometimes enemies and sometimes allies. At one time Nubian rulers had even sat on the throne of Egypt.

After Egypt became an Arab ally, Nubia was cut off from the rest of the Christian world. Still, it was not until the fifteenth century that Alodia, the southernmost kingdom in Nubia, was overrun by the Muslims. Nubia had been Christian for nine hundred years.

But not as long as Ethiopia. Ethiopia has a long and colorful history, mixed with elements of legends and myths. During the tenth century B.C., a dying Ethiopian king made his daughter, Makeda, his successor. She ruled as the queen of Sheba. According to Judeo-Christian scriptures, the queen of Sheba visited King Solomon's court in Jerusalem and established the long relationship between Ethiopia and the Judeo-Christian religions.

The thirteenth-century church at Lalibela, in modern-day Ethiopia. Trenches were dug down sixty feet into solid rock, leaving a pillar in the shape of a cross, which was then hollowed out to form the church.

Prester John, on his throne in east Africa. Detail from a Portuguese map of 1493.

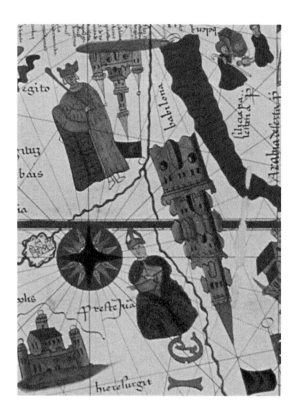

The legend of Prester John is another of the marvelous Ethiopian stories that's rooted in fact but sustained by myth.

Prester John was believed to be a priest-king over a vast Christian empire somewhere in east Africa. St. Thomas the Apostle was said to have designed Prester John's palace, which contained a mirror through which the great king could survey his kingdom. All manner of amazing creatures lived in his kingdom, among them a kind of salamander whose skin couldn't be burned. Prester John's robes were believed to have been made from salamander skin.

Over a long period of time, bits and pieces of this story reached Europe through Muslim Spain. Gradually, the legendary kingdom was identified as Ethiopia. This strange story was still circulating around southern Europe in the fifteenth century.

But with the rise of Islam, Axum (Ethiopia's commercial center on the Red Sea) had been cut off from the Christian world. Christianity survived in Axum through many centuries of conflict with its Arab neighbors.

When the Portuguese explorer Vasco da Gama arrived at Axum in the fifteenth century, he learned of the exotic churches of Lalibela, where people had been worshiping for a long, long time and the New Testament had been translated into the Ethiopian language, Geez. The Christianity practiced at Axum, however, was deeply rooted in ancient African, Jewish, and Christian rituals and traditions.

So when da Gama returned to Portugal with reports of locating a Christian kingdom in east Africa, many believed Prester John's empire had been found. The king of Portugal sent a military expedition to help defend Christian Ethiopia from invading Muslims. In fact, Vasco da Gama's son was killed during a battle there in 1504.

GHANA

Not all Muslim conquests were military, like the ones in Egypt, Ethiopia, and north Africa. Muslims also conducted peaceful, commercial *jihads,* wherein scholars, merchants, writers, and scientists spread their beliefs on a day-to-day basis. Arab travelers and traders brought the message of Islam to Ghana sometime in the eighth century.

Founded by the Soninke people, this Ghana—not to be confused with the present-day country of Ghana—was the first west African empire below the Sahara. It flourished between A.D. 700 and 1200 as an important trade and cultural center, the crossroads of the salt and gold trade.

Although Islam was advancing steadily, its influence was not widespread in Ghana. Outside the cities, the people continued to worship the serpent-spirit Ouagadou-Bida. But we owe a debt of gratitude to Arab writers and scholars like al-Bakri, an eleventh-century Spanish Moor from Córdoba, who left a written record of Ghana's splendor. In his *Book of Roads and Kingdoms,* al-Bakri wrote that the king of Ghana was "the wealthiest of all kings on the face of the earth."

In about 1052, the Almoravids, a fanatical Islamic group, began a series of attacks against Ghana's smaller city-states, plundering them and forcing many of the people to become Muslims. Although the Almoravids weren't able to maintain their power, they disrupted Ghana's imperial system, and after a series of devastating military defeats Ghana fell into a period of confusion and decline.

MALI

As old Ghana faced ruin, another kingdom rose out of its ashes. Many of the smaller states within the Ghanan Empire took advantage of this chaotic period and declared themselves independent. Among them were the Mandinka (Mandingo) people of the little kingdom of Mali.

The first of the Mali leaders was Sundiata, whose name means "hungering lion." Unlike the lion, Sundiata was born physically weak and lame. But with the loving help of his mother, the boy grew into a powerful and wise leader.

In 1235, Sundiata led a rebellion against the enemy of his people, Sumanguru, king of the Sosso. The two armies clashed at Karina. Sundiata emerged victorious. Koumbi, the last stronghold of Ghana's Soninke leaders, fell five years later, and Mali became the undisputed military, trade, and political power in the region for the next two hundred years.

Under King Sundiata's brilliant leadership Mali absorbed Ghana's principal trade centers and expanded into new territory. Mali also maintained a monopoly on the gold and salt trade. Sundiata organized the government and became a national hero. But the Malian ruler most respected, feared, and remembered was Mansa Kankan Musa I.

He ruled a kingdom roughly the size of western Europe. Sheik Uthman ed-Dukkali, an Egyptian who lived in Mali for thirty-five years, wrote that the empire was "four months' travel long and four months' wide."

Ibn Battuta, a Berber scholar and theologian from Tangier, crossed the Sahara in 1352 and spent about a year in the kingdom of Mali.

He observed that "the Africans are seldom unjust and have a greater abhorrence of injustice than any other people. . . . There is complete security in their country. Neither traveler nor inhabitant in it has anything to fear from robbers or men of violence."

Mansa Musa's critics noted that although he was a devout Muslim, he allowed his subjects to worship as they chose. And according to Battuta, even some of Mansa Musa's closest advisers were themselves religious "backsliders."

Knowledge of Mali's wealth and splendor startled Egypt and Arabia in 1324, when Mansa Musa made his *hadj*—a pilgrimage to

OPPOSITE: *A Mali horseman, crafted out of terra-cotta (a kind of hard-baked clay) around the fourteenth century.*

View of Timbuktu, three hundred years after the height of its glory in the fifteenth century. Notice the mixture of traditional African rounded structures and Arab-style square ones.

Mecca, the holy city of Islam. He entered the city with a sixty-thousand-man escort, including five hundred slaves, each of whom bore a bar of gold weighing four pounds. He used the gold to pay for his own expenses; then he gave the rest away to his various hosts and to the poor and needy. Mansa Musa gave away so much that Egypt's money market took twelve years to return to normal!

During Mansa Musa's *hadj*, the Malian army captured the city of Gao, the capital city of the Songhai people. On his return, Mansa Musa stopped by Gao to make a peace agreement with King Assibai. But just to make sure the king kept his word, Mansa Musa took two of Assibai's sons back to Niani, his capital, as permanent "guests."

After returning to Niani, located near the Niger River, the king ruled for many years, enjoying the benefits of his empire. Under him, great advancements in scholarship were made at Timbuktu. The city hadn't reached its peak yet, but even during Mansa Musa's time, no place could rival it in commerce or culture, not even Niani.

Leo Africanus, a Spanish Moor, got his name from Pope Leo X, when Africanus converted to Christianity in 1518. He'd fascinated the pope with stories about his travels to Africa in early 1500. The pope gave Africanus a pension so he could write the story of what he'd seen during his travels. He completed the first volume in 1526.

Of Timbuktu, Africanus wrote: "There are numerous judges, doctors, and clerics, all receiving good salaries from the King. He pays great respect to men of learning. . . . There is a big market for manuscript books from the Berber countries, and more profit is made from the sale of books than from any other merchandise."

A number of contemporary historians believe sailors from Mali might have reached the Americas during the reign of Mansa Musa, a full century before Columbus. But there is no conclusive proof.

SONGHAI

The year Columbus began his first voyage marked the decline of Mali. The Songhai Empire was the rising star in the western Sudan.

Remember the three Songhai princes who were taken back to Niani? When Mansa Musa died in 1332, the princes escaped and went back to Gao, where they established the Sunni dynasties.

In 1364, Sunni (Sonni) Ali the Great became Songhai's leader. He captured Timbuktu first and then Jenne, a well-fortified city located on the Niger River. Mansa Musa had attacked Jenne nine times and failed to take it. Sunni Ali's army captured Jenne in 1473, but the siege had lasted seven years, seven months, and seven days. The Jenne soldiers had impressed Sunni Ali with their loyalty and bravery so much that he ordered his men not to harm any of them.

Jenne became a well-known medical center of the Songhai Empire. Doctors advised women to space their children, having one every three years rather than too many too quickly. The mos-

The great mosque at Jenne, as it stands today.

quito was isolated as the cause of malaria, and doctors routinely removed cataracts from the human eye.

Sunni Ali loosely practiced Islam, but his critics reviled him because of his tolerance of other religions, even more so than Mansa Musa. Muslim biographers invariably regard him as an enemy of their faith, or at least of orthodoxy. In north Africa, however, he was regarded as the "greatest king south of the Sahara" in his day.

Sunni Ali's son succeeded him in 1492. But a soldier named Askia Muhammad held a military coup in 1493 and took over the government, establishing the Askia dynasty—Askia is a term that roughly means "warrior-king."

To show his devout obedience to Islam, Askia made a pilgrimage to Mecca and Medina equally as memorable as the one made by Mansa Musa. He returned home spiritually fulfilled and fired by the spirit to conduct a series of *jihads* against his neighbors. Songhai's military might, under the leadership of its warrior-king, secured its place as the number-one power in the Sudan for about a century.

Gao was to Songhai what Timbuktu was to Mali. Located on the Niger River, it became well known as a craftsman's paradise. Goldsmiths, leather workers, blacksmiths, weavers, and potters turned out exquisite pieces that brought fame and fortune to the city.

Askia heavily funded the universities at Gao, Timbuktu, and Jenne and encouraged research. Students took courses in astronomy, mathematics, ethnography, medicine, logic, music, and much more. The faculty's reputations were far reaching, too. Professor Ahmed Baba, a respected professor at Sankore in Timbuktu, wrote forty books and had sixteen hundred books in his personal library.

This is the world Askia Muhammad ruled for over forty years. He died on March 2, 1538, at the age of ninety-seven. He didn't live to see four thousand Moroccan soldiers charge out of the Sahara, scattering his once-mighty armies in all directions. Timbuktu and Jenne retained their traditions and practice of scholarship for a while. But by 1600 the Songhai Empire had disintegrated and had been absorbed by other states, such as the Hausa, Bornu, and Kanem, to name a few. But none of these kingdoms would glow quite as brightly as the great Ghana, Mali, and Songhai.

THE BERBERS

The invading Moroccans were a Berber people, so named by the Romans, who called all foreigners, including north Africans, *barbari*—"barbarians"—which later became Berber. They ruled the desert, using the sun, stars, and wind patterns to navigate through the desert.

Timbuktu, Gao, and Jenne became part of the great Berber-controlled trade system. Traveling in donkey and camel caravans, sometimes twelve thousand strong, Berber traders moved from one oasis to another, linking west Africa to north Africa, Egypt, and Arabia. They were capable of carrying gold, ivory, cloth, and salt across the Sahara Desert.

Originally *Sahra* (Sahara) was a thirsty man's plea for water. Later Sahara meant "desert." By the fifteenth century, Sahara named the three-million-square-mile desert in north Africa.

The Berbers were a nomadic people, and though they spoke a common language, each group was fiercely independent, loyal only to their kinsmen. They lived on the fringes of the ever-encroaching Sahara, which was harsh and unforgiving. So were the

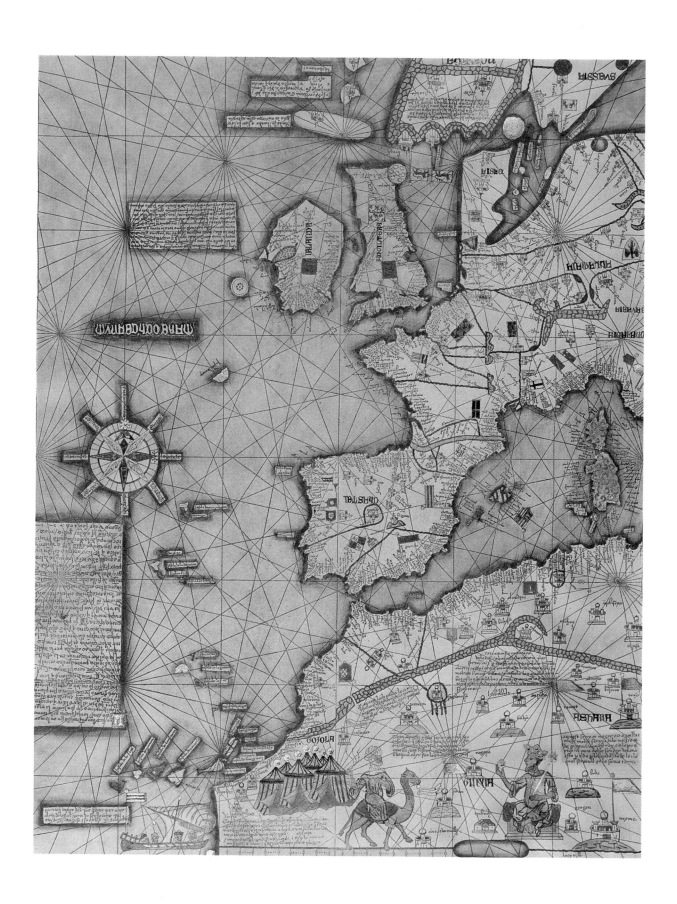

Berbers, by some standards. Mistakes cost lives, so they lived by a strict code of conduct, and offenders were shown little mercy.

The legendary Berber herdsmen raised camels and horses for the caravans and charged high prices for their stock. It's a wonder, because the camels were ornery beasts, ill-tempered, stubborn, and smelly. Even when tied down at night, camels sometimes escaped and wandered away, causing a day's delay while they were rounded up. These flea-ridden beasts of burden—sometimes called desert ships—made a long trip even longer, a hard trip harder. The only thing going for them was their endurance. No other animal could go as far and as long on less water.

The Berbers raised horses to sell, but they kept the best ones for themselves. The Berber horsemen were skilled riders, recognized by their magnificently crafted two-edged swords and sheathed daggers, iron lances, and leather shields. No wonder they were called the Lords of the Desert.

Among the Taureg Berbers, adult males wore blue veils in the presence of strangers, women, and in-laws. The dye rubbed off on their faces, leaving a blue tint. So they were known as the Blue Men of the North.

THE SWAHILI

While the Berbers fought their neighbors for control of the great trading cities along the Niger, the Swahili were the undisputed lords of east African sea trade. Gold, ivory, rare food, spices, iron, cloth, pottery, and even animals were traded at the busy markets in Kilwa, Mombasa, Sofala, Malindi, and Zanzibar or shipped to trading centers in India and China. A Swahili ruler sent a giraffe to the emperor of China in 1415.

The Swahili, whose trading empire flourished from the twelfth through the fifteenth centuries, had a high standard of living, which included indoor plumbing. They had a simple but just way of governing. Their king, known as Wafalme, which means Son of the Great Lord, was expected to rule justly. If he didn't, his people killed him and refused to allow any of his relatives to rule afterward. As an Arab writer observed, the Swahili "consider that in acting wrongfully [the king] forfeits his position as the son of the Lord, the king of Heaven and Earth."

OPPOSITE: *A European map of the fourteenth century includes northern Africa and the Sudan. The figure on the camel at bottom is a Taureg Berber. The seated figure with crown and scepter is the Malian king Mansa Musa.*

Women went to the marketplace every day with their babies strapped on their backs. It was a noisy but colorful place, full of laughter and chatter, shrill haggling, and, of course, gossip. The women bought their daily supply of fish, millet, and *kalari*—a plant much like the mushroom. They traded handmade baskets for cucumbers, honey, or rice. Since most meals included a banana dish, shoppers were always willing to pay a little more for the prized Indonesian variety than for the local banana crop. After the purchase, the women carried their goods home in baskets they carried gracefully on their heads. On the way they might sing, because Swahili is a musical language that invites a song.

The jewel of the Swahili port cities was Kilwa. Ibn Battuta, who also visited east Africa, wrote about the people. "We spent a night on the island [off Mombasa] and then set sail for Kilwa, the principal town on the coast, the greater part of whose inhabitants are Zanj of very black complexion. . . . Kilwa is one of the most beautiful and well-constructed towns in the world. The whole of it is elegantly built."

This Ming bowl, probably from the fifteenth century, was discovered in east Africa—evidence of centuries-old sea trade.

The gift of a Swahili ruler, a giraffe arrives in China. Detail of a Chinese painting recording the event.

The ruins of the mosque at Kilwa as they appear today.

When Vasco da Gama sailed around the Cape of Good Hope and up the eastern coast in 1497 and 1498, he found fleets of ships in the harbor at Kilwa, many of which were larger than his own caravel. Swahili sailors understood compasses and charts and had been navigating the seas, trading with India, Indonesia, Ceylon, China—and beyond—for centuries.

When da Gama returned to east Africa on his second voyage in 1502, he gave a detailed description of Kilwa. He said it was a city of great size, with "good buildings of stone and mortar with terraces, and . . . much wood works. The city comes down to the shore, and is entirely surrounded by a wall and towers, within which there may be twelve thousand inhabitants."

The Portuguese disrupted the Indian Ocean trade routes for their own purposes, causing the decline of the Swahili trading empires. The Portuguese burned and sacked Kilwa. Without hope or heart, the people never rebuilt it.

YORUBA

Although Islam played an important role in African cultures, countless others kept their traditional religions. For example, the Swahili called their god Maliknajlu, which means Great Lord. And the Yoruba, on the other side of the continent, worshiped Olodumare, the High God.

The Yoruba believed, for example, that Olodumare made the earth, then let Orishanla, a lesser god, complete the job, which included the creation of man.

The largest Yoruban states were Oyo and Ife, both located in the southwestern portion of what is now Nigeria. The Yoruba believed that mankind was created at Ife and from there spread all over the world. Oduduwa, the legendary hero of Yoruba and founder of Ife, made it the spiritual capital of his people. His ancestors were the first *alafins*, which meant "divine leaders."

The Yoruba loved and respected their *alafin*, who was their spiritual leader. Most Yoruba, however, lived in small, self-governed villages.

By the sixteenth century Yoruban farmers had mastered agricultural techniques and applied them to their special environments in the tropical forests. Their language and beliefs united them.

Religion directed the movement of their lives from life to death. Their language gave them a connection between the two. A rich oral tradition of stories and history was passed from one generation to another.

A Yoruban storyteller, usually the oldest person in the village, knew a wide range of oral literature with which to teach and entertain listeners. Storytellers carried village histories in their heads and had a story to fit every occasion, always quickly shared.

For example, children and adults loved the exploits of Ananse the Spider. And "why myths" like the following one helped explain the world around them:

> When Orishanla was making man, a jealous animal [can be any the storyteller chooses] tricked the young god into getting drunk on palm wine. That's why, according to the Yoruba, human beings are not perfect.

The storyteller used proverbs to pass on the collective wisdom of his people. This one is an example: "Peace is the father of friendship."

OPPOSITE: *Yoruban warrior in bronze.*

The Yoruba were famous for their riddles, too. Can you answer these?

- We tie a horse in the house, but its mane flies about the roof.
- Two tiny birds jump over two hundred trees.
- We call the dead—they answer. We call the living—they do not answer.

The answer to the first riddle is "fire and smoke." To the second, "a person's eyes—they can see far away." And the last answer is "walking on dead leaves that crunch, and walking on green leaves that don't."

The *oriki,* a praise-song, captured a person's good and bad deeds, successes and failures, and physical attributes in a musical poem.

Professional musicians sang the *orikis* of hosts, guests, and the gods at special functions. The most poetic *orikis* were dedicated to the gods. Here is an *oriki* to Oshun, one of the three river wives of Shango, the thunder god:

> She is rich and her words are sweet.
> Large forest and plenty of food.
> Let a child embrace my body.
> The touch of a child's hand is sweet.
> Owner of brass.
> Owner of parrots' feathers.
> Owner of money.
> My mother, you are beautiful, very beautiful.
> Your eyes sparkle like brass.
> Your skin is soft and smooth.
> You are black like velvet.
> Everybody greets you when you descend on the world.
> Everybody sings your praises.

Drum makers were honored citizens of the community, and so were drummers. All formal ceremonies began with the call of the "talking drums." Yoruban drummers were trained from birth. By the time they reached adulthood, they were highly skilled messengers who could talk to other drummers miles away by using the tonal patterns found in their spoken language.

Superstitions shaped many Yoruban attitudes. It wasn't uncommon to see a man holding a chewing stick while talking to a creditor. He was trying to ward off a pending quarrel. A new bride would lovingly place a bundle of feathers near her husband's sleeping mat to guard him against evil. And mothers twisted copper rings around their children's wrists to prevent snake bites.

At the core of an intricate pattern of religious ritual was ancestor veneration. To a new mother, her baby meant the rebirth of an older soul who'd come back to live again. Three months after a baby was born, the parents took him or her to an oracle. There the name of the reborn ancestor was revealed. Children were loved dearly, as this Yoruban poem suggests.

> A child is like a rare bird.
> A child is precious like coral.
> A child is precious like brass.
> You cannot buy a child on the market.

Several Yoruban states thrived during the fourteenth century, especially Oyo. The leader of Oyo was the most powerful, so he was given the *ida oranyan,* the sword of state. It symbolized his earthly and spiritual authority. In a long and complicated coronation, he promised never to attack the holy city of Ife. Afterward Ife remained the spiritual capital of the Yoruba, and Oyo its royal capital.

BENIN

Other people built empires in the forest belt along the coast of west Africa too. Among them were the Akawamu, Denkyira, Asante (Ashanti), and Benin. The Benin, located in present-day Nigeria, flowered between the thirteenth and the nineteenth centuries.

The Benin Empire was non-Yoruban, but it resembled the culture at Ife more so even than the Yoruban people of Oyo did.

Eweka was the first *oba* (king) of Benin. But Ewuare the Great was the most remembered because, unlike the neighboring Yoruba, Ewuare consolidated his political power at a central location, in Benin City. It remained the capital from 1140 to 1480.

Bronze statue of a Benin flute player.

Ewuare held on to his power against his adversaries because he was a warrior and a statesman, and some say a powerful magician. By most accounts Ewuare proved brave and wise.

The *oba* represented the Benin gods on earth. Anyone who challenged his authority was executed at once. The day-to-day business of the government was conducted by the king's trusted ministers. They carried on economic and military affairs in the *oba*'s name.

The king's numerous wives lived a few miles from Benin City, away from the political arena. But every month there was a festival of some kind. The king's fashionable wives, young princes and princesses, and nobles gathered in the *oba*'s court to eat and have fun. They played games, drank bamboo wine, danced, sang, announced marriages and births, passed out honors—and reprimands—and told stories.

The people of Benin, the Bini (Beny), had a network of oral literature comparable to that of the Yoruba. The king's counselor understood the power of stories when handling sensitive political matters. The king, who was considered a god-man, wouldn't be criticized by anyone. Questioning a royal decision openly could mean death, so ministers used stories like this one to instruct, persuade, or convince their king:

> "Once there was a cruel king who ordered his subjects to build a new palace from the top downward." The storyteller asked his audience how they would solve the problem. Then he continued. "A wise man came along and suggested that the king—in accordance with tradition—should be given the honor of laying the first stone. Of course, any change of plan was the king's idea."

The climax of these monthly affairs was human sacrifice. The Bini believed in a supreme god whom they didn't need to worship. But the lesser gods, especially those who had the power to disrupt daily life, had to be appeased. Victims rarely struggled, and some even volunteered to be sacrificed, which suggests that their religious beliefs were intense indeed.

Craftsmen left detailed records of Benin life in art. Benin sculptors had no equals. A series of bronze plaques, commissioned by the *oba* to adorn the pillars of his palace, are as much a tribute to the Bini craftsmen as they are to the civilization they depicted.

OPPOSITE: *Bronze wall plaque, from Benin. The king wears elaborate necklaces and other jewelry and is shaded from the sun by his retainers.*

The coming of the Europeans was recorded in Benin art. Here is a brass figure of a Portuguese soldier.

According to artistic representations, the Benin were a highly organized society. Among their prestigious citizens were the hunters—the providers of the kingdom.

Most boys grew up wanting to be hunters, but only a few managed to qualify as apprentices. When a boy turned thirteen or fourteen, an older hunter began training him physically and mentally. First the young apprentice learned to track game in different terrains and to move quietly and quickly through thorny underbrush. Sometimes the young hunter was required to stalk his prey for days, staying in the forest for long periods without food.

Trainees who survived this part progressed to the next stage. The boys had to learn the hunters' secret language and magical rituals. One special ceremony was supposed to make a hunter invisible to his prey.

After years of hard work, dedication, and discipline, the young man was welcomed into the brotherhood of hunters, a great honor. But even among their peers, the elephant hunters were considered the masters.

These legendary men gathered early in the morning, armed with blowguns, poisoned darts, and magic charms. Their work was dangerous, with very little margin for error. Several days—sometimes weeks—later they would return with an elephant, which provided enough meat to feed everybody and ivory to trade.

Customarily one of the elephant's tusks went to the *oba;* the man responsible for the kill received the other, along with the head, heart, and lungs, which were considered powerful charms.

Standing beside the hunters in society were the soldiers—the defenders of the kingdom. The *oba*'s generals boasted that they could raise one hundred thousand soldiers in a day. Whether that's true isn't known, but the Benin armies were a formidable military force in the forest region.

Ranked next in the social order were craftsmen, farmers, then slaves. It's interesting that Benin slaves could advance through work; also they could buy their freedom or earn it through outstanding service or good fortune, such as inheriting goods or marrying into the master's family. Sometimes a master might marry one of his slaves or adopt one as a daughter or son. Through such means it was not at all unusual for former slaves to acquire positions of great influence and power in Benin.

The Portuguese made contact with the Benin in 1486. Ruy de

Pina, a court historian, related what happened: "The king of Beny [Benin] sent an ambassador to the king of Portugal, a negro, one of his captains, from a harboring place by the sea, which is called Ugato [Gwato]. This ambassador was a man of good speech and natural wisdom. Great feasts were held in his honor, and he was shown many of the good things of these kingdoms. He returned to his land in a ship. . . . But owing to the fact that the land was afterward found to be very dangerous from sickness and not so profitable as had been hoped, the trade was abandoned."

THE KINGDOM OF THE CONGO

The Dutch, and later English, explorers followed the Portuguese down the west coast of Africa. British sailors sang this song about the Guinea Coast, also called the Bight of Benin:

> Beware and take care
>   of the Bight of Benin:
> For each one that comes out
>   there are forty go in.

Portuguese soldiers arrange themselves into square formations in battle with an Angolan army. The Angolans were neighbors of the Congolese.

Fear of this region was not without reason. When the Portuguese explorer Diego Cão tested the waters below the Bight of Benin in 1482, his crew threatened mutiny. The blue-green water stayed calm until they moved south of Gabon. The farther south he traveled, the choppier the water became. Contrary winds and powerful currents jostled his caravel around like a child's toy boat.

At last Cão's ship came to the mouth of an uncharted river pouring into the Atlantic. Cão's men watched in amazement as they sailed upriver, past vine-covered trees standing like giant sentinels guarding this unknown world. The place tingled with life—squealing monkeys, squawking birds, buzzing insects. Crocodiles greeted them with menacing smiles. The smell of decaying wood and rotting vegetation hung heavy in the hot and humid air.

Cão didn't know it, but he was sailing up the Zaire (Congo) River, slipping deeper and deeper into the heart of the Congo.

The kingdom of the Congo and its connection with the Portuguese remains one of the most tragic stories of the sixteenth century.

Cão went back to Portugal with stories about what he'd seen. In 1490, runners hurried to tell the Mani-Congo (a name for the ruler) that a group of white men were sailing up the Zaire. With the expedition were soldiers, priests, missionaries, craftsmen, and even women.

King Nizinga Mbemba was pleased. He welcomed the Portuguese and opened his kingdom to them. At first the Congolese and Portuguese accepted each other. They had a common interest in trading. The captain added weapons to the trading list in exchange for captives whom he might take back with him. The king offered him twenty or thirty prisoners of war.

Two years later, Columbus's voyage ushered in the age of exploration and opened the Americas for European colonization. The rich soil and long growing season of South America and the Caribbean encouraged agricultural development. Although Pope Leo X had issued a papal bull (declaration) in 1514 against slavery, the traffic in human lives flourished. Slave labor was used to produce the first sugarcane crop in Brazil, in 1532. The slaves, more than likely, came from the Congo.

King Mbemba was baptized a Christian and renamed Dom Affonso (Alfonso). He was taught how to read and write, and he encouraged his subjects to do the same. With the help of Portuguese soldiers and their superior weapons, Affonso defeated his enemies. All captives were taken away in the Portuguese ships.

In spite of Affonso's cooperation with the Portuguese in providing large numbers of captives for the slave market, the demand for slaves exceeded the supply. So the Portuguese began taking Affonso's people.

He wrote to Dom João, king of Portugal in 1526: "Sir, Your Highness should know how our Kingdom is being lost in so many ways. . . . Merchants are taking every day our natives, sons of the land and the sons of our noblemen and vassals and our relatives."

Affonso asked the king to "not agree with this nor accept it as in your service." But the door had been opened to the slavers, and they weren't willing to leave. In fact, the raids increased. Affonso sent a group of young men to be educated in Portugal only to find out later that they had been enslaved. Even some of the Portuguese priests in the Congo entered the slave trade.

Affonso wrote another passionate letter in 1526 asking the Portuguese king for physicians, apothecaries, and a surgeon. In the

King Affonso receiving a Portuguese delegation, as imagined by a French historian some seventy years after the event.

same year he asked the king to send "neither merchants nor wares," but "priests, and people to teach in schools, and no other goods but wine and flour for the sacrament."

Still his request was ignored. Ships came, but they came for slaves. As the evils of the slave trade ravaged his empire, Affonso died brokenhearted and betrayed.

The Congolese people split into warring factions, with the Portuguese slavers taking captives from both sides. Thousands of men, women, and children were herded onto slave ships and transported to the New World. By 1667 the Congo had been sacked; the Portuguese had taken all they could.

AFTER COLUMBUS

Close to twelve million slaves were taken out of Africa to work on plantations in Brazil, the West Indies, Central America, Mexico,

Some of the ruins of Great Zimbabwe.

and the United States. Many millions more perished. And to justify the deed, slavers claimed Africans were savages, inferior beings, incapable of producing anything worthy of recognition. But the slavers knew better. When Columbus was on his fourth and last voyage to the New World, the Karanga, a Bantu-speaking people in southeast Africa, were adding new buildings to Great Zimbabwe, an urban center spreading over six hundred acres.

When Columbus was spending a year marooned in Jamaica, Zimbabwe craftsmen were smelting gold and silver and carving birds out of soapstone.

And when Columbus died in Spain in 1506, the people of Zimbabwe were using copper coins to buy fine porcelain from China.

Yet when eighteenth-century archeologists found the ruins of Great Zimbabwe, they refused to believe they were the ruins of an advanced African civilization. The deliberate distortion and destruction of Africa had been so thorough that it was easier for them to suggest that visitors from outer space had built the city than to credit Africans with the knowledge and ability necessary to develop it.

Contrary to what the world came to believe after 1492, Africa was not a "dark continent" waiting for someone to bring the light. Africa is too big, too old, and too diverse to be so narrowly defined.

AUSTRALIA AND OCEANIA IN 1492
Margaret Mahy

Let your eye wander across Asia, down through India, and along the Malay Peninsula, which points like a crooked finger to the broken patchwork of islands that we now call Indonesia. Look past the big islands of Sumatra, Java, and Borneo, past the smaller islands of the Celebes, and you will find another large island—New Guinea. New Guinea, together with its neighbors Vanuatu, New Caledonia, the Solomon Islands, and Fiji, makes up an area called Melanesia.

To the north of New Guinea lie whole families of islands—the Marianas, the Marshall Islands, the Caroline Islands, and the Gilberts—all small islands, which is why this group is called Micronesia. Further east lies an area shaped like an arrowhead. Easter Island marks the tip of the arrowhead. Hawaii and New Zealand are the points at its base. Within this triangle lie Tonga, the Cook Islands, the Tokelaus, Samoa, and small island groups such as the Marquesas, the Society Islands, the Tuamoto Islands, and Tahiti. This triangle aimed at the side of South America is called Polynesia. West of the Polynesian Islands and south of Melanesia you will find the biggest island in the world, an island so big it is more than an island, it is a continent as well. This is the country of Australia. To the east of Australia lie the three islands of New Zealand, a country that looks like a small, eager animal twisting and leaping beside its great companion.

Together all these islands make up a part of the world that is called Oceania because the islands lie within the Pacific Ocean, an ocean so big that it covers a third of the earth's surface.

HISTORY, WHISPERS, STORIES, AND GOSSIP

We can ask what was going on in parts of Africa or the Americas or Asia or Europe five hundred years ago, and we can find some sort of account or description of events and of the people who were alive then. The 1400s saw the beginning of a great phase of exploration, as the countries of western Europe looked east.

For many years goods from India and the islands that are now part of Indonesia had come across land to Europe by Arab trade routes. Silks, carpets, rare woods, and spices came in through Venice and Genoa and other Mediterranean ports. But in the 1400s the old trade routes fell under the domination of the Turkish Ottoman Empire, which was hostile to Europe. Spain and Portugal were growing jealous of Venice, which had controlled the valuable spice trade for so long. They began to send out explorers, hoping to find a way to trade directly with the Spice Islands, for the trade in spice and pepper was extremely valuable. These explorers brought back stories, partly imagined and partly true, of fabulous lands on the edge of the world.

But most of the islands of Oceania were so far away from Europe that they were not even whispered about. The people who lived in Oceania in the fifteenth century did not travel north, and most of them did not keep written records. They *remembered* their legends and histories and told them to one another and then to their children. Their history is a sort of poetry. It emphasizes a different truth from the truth we expect to find in a written history, but we must pay attention to it just as we would to any history.

THE ICE AGE

The most popular view today is that the whole human race originally came out of Africa and slowly spread through Europe and Asia, then down through Indonesia and into the islands of the Pacific Ocean. Moving around the world in the days before recorded history, people left traces behind them, and nowadays we try to follow these prehistoric trails. We puzzle over the clues and often argue about them. Going by the color of skin, the amount of curl in hair, the shapes of faces and heads, and other clues of this kind, we put people in different groups, calling them Asian or

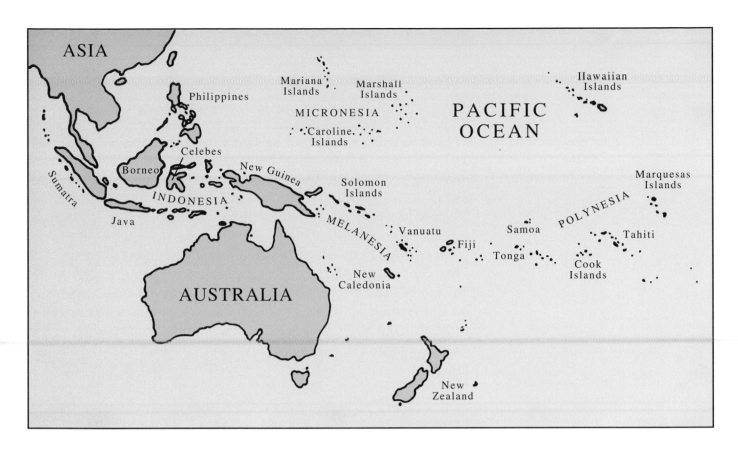

Polynesian or Melanesian according to their general physical appearance. Some communities may behave in similar ways. Do they make gardens, we ask? Do they farm and domesticate animals? Do they make pottery? Are they warriors? What are their beliefs? Do they share the same stories? The answers to these questions also suggest that certain peoples are related to one another in some way. Language is important too. Physical appearance, culture, and language may not prove anything on their own, but they help us build a pattern, and patterns suggest the answers to many puzzles.

A hundred and twenty-five thousand years ago, the world was in the grip of an ice age. Ice advanced across Europe and Canada. There were glaciers in Tasmania and New Zealand and even in Hawaii. More than seventeen million cubic miles of water had frozen and was locked up in great masses of ice.

Even a huge ocean like the Pacific is affected by the loss of so much water, so it was a time of lower sea levels around the world. In fact, the water level was probably about four or five hundred feet lower than it is today, and the islands that stretch from Malaysia through Indonesia and the Philippines were joined together.

Thousands of years ago a small, dark, frizzy-haired people moved out of Asia, down through Indonesia, and into the Pacific. They were not gardeners or farmers, but they must have been able to travel by sea, even if at that time they did not have to travel far. Their journey south was a slow one, probably taking place over many years. The descendants of these early inhabitants are still found living inland in places such as Papua and the Solomon Islands. However, Oceania was mostly populated by a later group, the Austronesians.

Lower sea levels do not entirely explain the spread of the Austronesians. Many of them became practiced ocean goers. Traveling in canoes and possibly (in the beginning) on bamboo rafts, they moved farther and farther south, going from one island group to another, even though some of these island groups, or archipelagoes, are separated by hundreds of miles of open sea.

INDONESIA

On the edge of Oceania is modern Indonesia, the biggest island group in the world. These islands are spread over three million square miles. However, if we add all the islands together, we get only 784,000 square miles of land. Indonesia is mostly sea. The biggest islands are Kaltimantan (Indonesian Borneo), Sumatra, Irian, Sulawesi (Celebes), and Java, and they hold about 90 percent of the population. But there are thousands of smaller islands, such as Maluku (once called the Moluccas).

Ten thousand years ago people with a food-gathering culture lived in Java, Sumatra, and the Celebes. There are signs of settlement by human beings related to the Melanesian-Papuan family group, a hunting and fishing and mollusk-gathering community, who were also in the process of setting up jungle gardens and planting yams and taros. This way of life lasted for about five thousand years. Then other people began to drift in from the north, people we can identify with the Indonesians of today. They probably came in a series of small advances, moving in over hundreds of years, rather than in a single invasion. They tended to occupy river mouths and coastal plains rather than inland areas, and they were traders. However, trading customs were not the only things they brought with them. They also brought rice.

Under pressure from this steady advance, the original population shifted to the interiors of the islands. Something of that ancient pattern exists today—there is a difference between the coastal people and those who live inland.

About two thousand years ago, these river-mouth settlements grew into a series of small states that traded with India and China, charged tolls, and even forced merchant ships to visit their ports whether they wanted to or not. By the fifth century A.D. these states were well established and were strongly influenced by Indian culture.

Trade leads to an exchange not only of goods but of ideas. Archeologists find signs of Indian art, architecture, and even mythology in the remains the people of these times left behind.

Various ports in southeast Sumatra developed into a confederation called Srivijaya, an empire based on international trade. Between the seventh and twelfth centuries, Srivijaya generally dominated not only the Straits of Malacca but the Malay Penin-

Seafaring ship, carved on the temple of Borobudur, Java.

sula, Sumatra, and the western part of Java. The powerful Buddhist Sailendra dynasty built the famous Borobudur victory monument in the center of Java. However, by the twelfth century Srivijaya was beginning to lose its power, partly because rival ports that were cheaper to use were developing in north Java.

Java had also developed its Indianized states. Most notable were Kalinga, a Hindu kingdom that was the center of culture and political power in about A.D. 700. Over the next three hundred years, the center of power, or *kraton*, shifted from one place to another in Java. Historians think that Java was made up of a group of small states linked together and yet all competing with one another to become the most powerful. Unlike those of the Srivijaya in Sumatra, these states had an agricultural base. The cultivation of *sawa*, or wet rice, in fertile volcanic soils was an important part of their commercial life.

In about 1222 a state called Singhasari became particularly powerful and rich through trade. In the late thirteenth century an emperor named Kartanagara extended the influence of Singhasari, taking over Madura and Bali and finally destroying Srivijaya. Perhaps this made Kartanagara overconfident. At least he felt powerful enough to reject the imperial envoys of China when they visited him. Kublai Khan, the emperor of China, was angry at the insult to his envoys and sent out a force to punish Kartanagara, but since he was dead by the time the emperor's force arrived, they took their revenge by overthrowing Singhasari's current ruler. This allowed a son-in-law of Kartanagara, Vija; to set up his *kraton* at a place called Majapahit. The Majapahit era saw the establishment of a commercial empire that included Borneo, Sumatra, the Malay Peninsula, and parts of the Philippines. It is still remembered as being particularly splendid and successful.

The *kraton* at Majapahit was abandoned in 1468, shortly before Columbus's famous journey. The north of Java was becoming increasingly important, and an entrepôt port arose at Malacca. Entrepôt ports were centers where exports and imports were stored and distributed. During this time the Hindu influence from India, which had been important for so long, was in retreat. Muslim culture was taking over.

Arab traders had been visiting Javanese ports for hundreds of years, and local people were no doubt influenced by Muslim ideas partly because of the ideas themselves and partly because the trade

OPPOSITE: *The great Buddhist temple at Borobudur on the island of Java. The temple was constructed over a thousand years ago.*

was so valuable. Sumbabwa, the Malay language of trade, was commonly used around the coasts. States like Perlak and Pasi in north Sumatra had been converted by 1300, and by 1535 most of the north coast of Java was Muslim. In 1492 this movement toward Muslim ideas was one of the important alterations that was taking place in the islands that are now part of the country of Indonesia.

The people of Java and Sumatra did not know that Columbus was trying to reach their part of the world. However, within ten years of Columbus's voyage, Europeans who had sailed around Africa began to arrive at their islands. Indeed, in 1511 the Portuguese captured the emporium of Malacca, a great distribution area, and in 1521 the Spanish fleet reached Tidore. They found there what Columbus would have found if he had ever reached the Indies. They were on the threshold of a zone much vaster and more mysterious than they had ever imagined.

MELANESIA

New Guinea and its neighboring island groups—the Solomons, the New Hebrides, New Caledonia, and, far to the east, Fiji—form the area now known as Melanesia.

The Melanesians are a very dark, frizzy-haired people, though there is a great variety of skin coloring among them. The inland people are small and stocky compared with coastal and swamp people, who came in later waves of settlement.

There are a wide variety of Melanesian people, but we should not be too surprised at that. Melanesia is an area of great contrasts. An astonishing variety of birds and insects flourish in these islands. There are many different landforms and climates, too. Melanesia is close to the equator, and certainly some parts of it are steamy and tropical. However, there are also mountainous zones that are damp and cool. It may be partly because of this variety of landscape and climate that Melanesian communities differ so widely from one another, but there are other reasons too.

Modern research shows that people were certainly living in New Guinea twenty-seven thousand years ago, and archeologists suspect they were there much earlier, particularly as there seem to be remote connections with the native Australians, who have been in

Australia for forty thousand years. Though the first Melanesians were hunters and gatherers, there are signs that in the central highlands of New Guinea people were gardening and keeping pigs as long as ten thousand years ago. However, very little is known about the Melanesians of these early days.

The Papuan people, the first inhabitants, spoke a language some forms of which still exist in the mountainous inland areas of New Guinea and in the Solomon Islands. These hunter-gatherers moved around rather than living in villages. But about five to six thousand years ago and possibly earlier, village-dwelling people came down into Melanesia, bringing new skills with them. They made pottery. They cultivated bananas, taros, yams, and coconuts, and also domesticated pigs, dogs, and the Indonesian jungle fowl. The new people were speakers of Austronesian and, as well as being gardeners, were ocean travelers. They took over the coastal areas of islands like New Guinea, forcing the Papuan-speaking people to move inland. As the centuries went by, New Guinea, like so much of Melanesia, became a place of numerous diverse peoples and languages. Partly because many of the communities developed separately, having little contact with their neighbors, hundreds of languages, some of them spoken by only a few thousand people,

This prehistoric stone carving, believed to be of Papuan origin, was found in the western highlands of New Guinea.

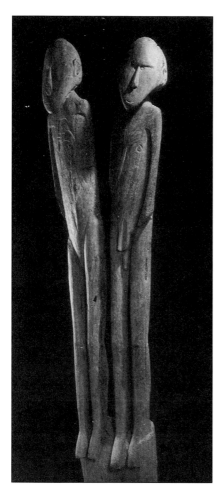

A carving representing male and female ancestors. From New Guinea.

slowly developed. Some villages to this day speak languages that do not seem to be related to the main language groups. This makes it hard for communities to talk to one another, and perhaps that is why it is so much a part of Melanesian culture to mistrust strangers. This hostility may have developed because the villages were so isolated. On the other hand, the isolation may have developed because people preferred to live and work in small groups connected partly through local trade but mainly through marriages.

Though some Melanesians did travel, they were not ambitious seafarers in the way that Polynesians were. But they did trade by sea, for travel by water was easier than travel by land. Thus the shore-dwelling Melanesians tended to pass their culture from one island to another, whereas inland communities were cut off, both by geography and by their suspicion of visitors. Their religious life was tied to a strong belief in magic. Rather than worship their gods and spirits, they tried to find ways and rituals with which to control them. Trade with coastal groups led some inland communities to develop ceremonial cycles and trade rituals that connected them to their neighbors. Through these rituals they might join together for wars or celebrations, but mostly they kept apart.

In 1492 Melanesians lived diverse lives in villages, fishing and working in gardens, some of which shifted from place to place according to the seasons. It was a hard life. People had to fight not only against the rugged land and the weather but against insect plagues and a wide variety of parasites, as well as illnesses such as malaria, blackwater fever, and leprosy. Indeed, the Melanesians of the past had to struggle so hard against nature that they wasted little time in struggling against one another. One village might raid a neighboring village, but the Melanesians were not empire builders and did not fight incessant wars, as some Polynesians did. Instead, they looked after their families and, year after year, cultivated yams, bananas, taros, and coconuts. The cultivation of rice had not spread to Melanesia.

Villages organized themselves according to many different systems. Food counted as wealth to the highland villagers. The family that had the most food in any year also had the most prestige, and the father of the family would be the "big man." However, "big man" status was not passed on to children. They had to win it for themselves. The "big man" could not store his surplus food for long. He could not save it as people save money. Instead, he would use his surplus to provide feasts, which added to his status in the eyes of his village. On the other hand, in a few communities, like those of the Trobriand Islanders, chieftainships could be inherited.

The Austronesian-speaking people were not only the ancestors of many Melanesian peoples, but possibly of the Polynesians, too. Some early Austronesians fished with spears and fish traps and built canoes up to sixty-five feet long with double hulls and sails woven of pandanus leaves. Their particular sort of pottery, lapita pottery, can be traced as they spread through what is now called New Ireland and New Britain, through the Solomon Islands and New Caledonia. By 1300 B.C. they were as far east as Fiji, probably the first people in this island group. Three hundred years later, they had reached well beyond the islands of Melanesia, to Tonga and possibly Samoa as well.

FIJI

In the days of Columbus, the Fijians were also putting out to sea, in large double-hulled canoes, sailing from their islands to Tonga and Samoa.

Fiji is made up of a group of about three hundred islands, many of which are quite small. The two largest, Viti Levu and Vanua Levu, make up between them 87 percent of the land area of Fiji. These big islands are covered in trees and include areas of tropical rain forest.

Physically, Fijians, with their frizzy hair and dark skins, resembled Melanesian people, and Fiji must count as part of Melanesia. However, their culture and customs were largely Polynesian. They had a plentiful food supply and developed a lively society with many crafts, including the making of paperbark cloth, wonderfully carved wooden weapons, and pottery that was much admired by their neighbors on Tonga. These items were part of their trade. Because they had access to timber, Fijians made particularly successful double-hulled canoes, which the Tongans also admired, envying the Fijians their access to valuable forests and their seagoing capacity.

Fijians worked hard at developing their land, terracing hillsides where necessary, bridging rivers, and building stone docks for their canoes.

Culturally they were fierce people. The Polynesians were often warlike, and war was certainly a part of Fijian culture. However, Fijian village customs were fierce too. Wives of dead chiefs were buried with them, and the old and infirm were often killed. Nevertheless there was much cooperation among various Fijian communities. They lent each other manpower when it was needed and exchanged natural resources such as fish, salt, woven mats, and canoe timbers. This system of support greatly helped the outer islands, which did not have the rich resources of the big islands in the center. If hurricanes damaged a particular island, recovery was usually swift thanks to inter-island cooperation. Fijian society was organized as a series of social groups with a chief at each level. At the heart of the system was a small federation of communities led by a chief who claimed supernatural connections. Through the person of this chief, ancient guardians of the land emerged to enrich the land and maintain its fertility. These gods, working through the chiefs, also took care of the community, so naturally the Fijians looked after their chiefs most carefully. A chief was set apart and surrounded by rituals, and anyone who insulted the chief insulted his people, too.

MICRONESIA

Micronesia is a wide area of sea scattered with very small islands. Nobody knows very much about the beginnings of human settlement there. Its islands are clustered into four main groups. The Marianas, as they are called today, are the most northerly. The Marshall Islands lie to the north of the equator, too, and the Gilberts to the south.

The people living in Micronesia are mostly Polynesian in appearance, although the inhabitants of the fourth island group, the Carolinas, tend to be shorter and darker, which suggests a Melanesian influence.

The Marianas are the islands where the Italian explorer Ferdinand Magellan landed in 1521, probably on Guam, after his famous voyage around Cape Horn. Here, and on Yap and Palau, too, Melanesian characteristics show up in the populations, along with some Asian ones. Archeologists think that the Mariana Islands were occupied as early as 1500 B.C. and that there might have been a second invasion of settlement in about A.D. 500. Because the islands are small and widespread, the first Micronesians must have been ocean-going voyagers, part of the flow of people who first brought the making of pottery to Melanesia.

POLYNESIA

Whereas the people of Melanesia were varied, Polynesian communities, even when separated by many thousands of miles of ocean, were often very similar to one another. The people resembled each other physically—tall, brown-skinned, with black hair that was wavy rather than frizzy. Connections can still be traced between the languages of islands as far apart as Easter Island, Tahiti, and New Zealand. Their folk tales and legends have a family resemblance. The trickster Maui, part man, part god, appears in the myths of many Polynesian islands.

Polynesians can be divided into two main groups—those from western Polynesia, which includes Tonga and Samoa, and those from eastern Polynesia, an area that includes Tahiti, the Marquesas, and Hawaii. Tahiti and Samoa are separated by about a thousand miles, while the distance between Samoa and the Marquesas is about two thousand miles. However, Polynesian travelers successfully covered these distances and made homes on all the southern islands of Oceania.

POLYNESIAN TRAVELERS

We can guess at the history of Polynesian movement from island to island because we find signs of the tools they used and the plants they grew. Reading the patterns of ocean currents, waves, and stars, they set out into the unknown, confident that somewhere out in the huge sea around them they would find land. *Kaveinga* was the name these early travelers had for the guiding stars. Knowing that certain stars passed directly over their home islands allowed these explorers to travel far into unknown seas and to find their way home again.

We don't know quite why these travelers set out. Possibly they were overcrowded on their own islands. On some occasions they may have been driven out by war. Sometimes a certain man would be sent into exile on the ocean, but would take food and his family with him, hoping that his skills would help him find a new land. Some Polynesian journeys were probably made by accident, but the first inhabitants of New Zealand, for instance, brought plants with them, as well as a native dog and a Polynesian rat, or *kiore*. We think they must have known they would be at sea for a long time, for they stocked their canoes or *whakas* well.

TONGA AND SAMOA

Tonga was one of the first islands to be occupied by Polynesians. There were people living there more than two thousand years ago, which is not so very long compared to the long history of settlement in Australia and parts of Melanesia. Nevertheless, the origin myths of Tonga do not tell of traveling and journeys, as do the first stories of the New Zealand Maori. Instead they tell about Maui and Tangaloa, who is not one god but several. Maui fished Tongatapu from the ocean floor. (In New Zealand folklore, Maui, using the South Island for a canoe, fished up the North Island.)

The Tongans were not isolated in the way some Polynesian communities were. They put out to sea, visiting Samoa and particularly Fiji, and may have learned some of their weapon-making skills from the Fijians.

Tangaloa, in one of his forms (Tangaloa Eitumatupu), was the father of the first king of Tonga, Aho'eitu, the Tu'i Tonga. This first king is the hero of a legend, but he seems also to have been a real man who lived about A.D. 950 and founded a Tongan dynasty that ruled for a thousand years. At the time of Columbus's voyage, the descendant of the Tu'i Tonga Aho'eitu was ruling not only Tonga but Samoa as well, as an earlier Tu'i Tonga, ruling around A.D. 1250, had invaded Samoa.

All over the world, royal and ruling families found themselves leading complicated lives. In approximately 1470, when Columbus was about twenty years old, there was intrigue and treachery at the court of the Tongan king. Kau'ulufonuafekai, the Tu'i Tonga of the time, gave the government over to his younger brother,

Takalaua, though he kept the spiritual part of the kingship in his own family. Takalaua became head of a clan called the Tu'i Ha'atatakalaua. Later a third kingly line was established, but conflicts arose among them. By the time the Europeans arrived, the structure of rule in Tonga was losing its traditional form as the three lines struggled among themselves to establish authority and power. Nevertheless the system had worked well. It had held the Tongans together as a people, and they had not found it necessary to build the sort of fortified villages that developed in New Zealand during the fifteenth century.

Like the Tongans and the New Zealanders, Samoans had a story of a trickster god called Maui, who in their version stole fire for mankind from the underworld. Unlike the people of many other Polynesian islands, Samoans do not begin their history with the story of a voyage; their stories are closer to the stories of Tonga. Ordinary persons were descended from worms that crawled out of rotten vines, but the chiefs were descended from the god Tangaloa. According to legend, Samoans have always lived on Samoa. However, archeological evidence suggests the island was settled only about a thousand years ago.

Samoan chiefs were called *matais*. Like Maori people, Samoans have complex family trees, and an extended family could share certain titles that brought privileges to the man who held them. It was usually a man who held the title, and though occasionally women might do so, this was most unusual. When the title holder died, the title was passed on or split up among his heirs.

Samoans lived in a relatively crowded part of the Pacific and traveled back and forth between Samoa, Tonga, Fiji, and the Tokelaus. They also received visits from other island travelers. In fact, at the time of Columbus's voyage, Samoa was actually ruled by Tongans.

THE MARQUESAS, TAHITI, HAWAII, AND EASTER ISLAND

Tahiti, the Marquesas, the Tuamotos, the Gambiers, and the Society Islands are all part of what is now called French Polynesia. The Tuamotos are coral atolls—islands made up of the accumulated skeletons of millions of years of coral growth. The other islands are volcanic in origin. The Marquesas were probably settled first, in about the second century A.D., by Polynesians from Samoa and Tonga. Having found the Marquesas and settled there, they then moved on to Tahiti, Hawaii, and Easter Island.

Northeast of Tahiti, at a distance of about 740 miles, lie twelve tall islands, the Society Islands, which are thought to be the jumping-off place for the Polynesian travelers who found their way to the Cook Islands and New Zealand.

The prehistory of the Marquesas is mostly in the form of stories that tell of continual wars between tribes. In fact, these wars were so persistent that they prevented any chance of unity among the islands. Nevertheless, the Marquesans attained a highly cultured stage. Their carvings, used to decorate houses and temples, are particularly beautiful.

The archipelagoes of Tahiti and distant Hawaii seem to have been settled at about the sixth or seventh century A.D., probably by Polynesians sailing from the Marquesas in double-hulled canoes. Later Tahitians sailed to Hawaii too, covering twenty-eight hundred miles of open sea. The Tahitian islands are not particularly good for gardeners, but the people ate coconut, mango, and breadfruit, and fished the many large species of fish that lived in the lagoons and open sea.

Though no one family completely dominated Tahiti, some families were highly respected because of their great family trees. Indeed, Tahitian societies were very ordered and complex. The ruling class was treated with great respect by the subchieftains and common people. They had their sacred ground, the *marae* (a word that is also found in the Maori language). The eastern Polynesians may have been separated from one another by hundreds of miles of ocean, but they are closely linked through culture and language.

Hawaii is made up of eight volcanic islands, the biggest of which also bears the name Hawaii. Having been geographically isolated for so long, these islands are remarkable for a range of plants that grow nowhere else. We think of Hawaii as tropical, which means it should be not only hot but wet and steamy too, and yet parts of it are dry enough for cactus to grow comfortably. It has only two native mammals—a kind of bat and a kind of seal—though the Polynesians introduced the rat, the dog, and the pig.

The first Hawaiians probably came from the Marquesas in the seventh or eighth century A.D. Another influx followed from

OPPOSITE: *Monumental statue on Easter Island, the easternmost Polynesian settlement.*

Tahiti in about A.D. 1200. As in Tahiti, family trees or genealogies were important and determined who the chiefs of the villages would be. In the beginning the Hawaiians lived in separate communities, some on low land and others in valleys, but intermarriage over a number of generations eventually united certain islands (Hawaii, Oahu, Maui, and Kauai) under one ruler. Their gods were Kane, the great creator; Ku, the god of war; and Kanaloa, the god of the sea. It is interesting to compare these names with the names of the Maori gods—Tane is the creator god, the god of the forest; Tu is the god of war; and Tangaroa is the god of the sea.

Because they had no written language, knowledge of Hawaiians—their history and stories of themselves—was contained in the form of chants, or *mele,* which were accompanied by dances. It was important for this knowledge to be remembered and passed on, and the chants and dances were formally taught. Music was important to the Hawaiians for religious reasons, but it was for pleasure and entertainment, too. Though they used percussion instruments such as drums and rattles, they had stringed instruments as well. When children were born, when boys officially became men, and when people died, these important occasions were marked by religious chants and dancing.

Easter Island was a remote Polynesian settlement, an island made up of three volcanic craters. Within the craters were lakes, which were important sources of fresh water, there being no permanent streams on Easter Island. Like many Polynesian peoples, the Easter Islanders respected their ancestors. They built about a thousand remarkable statues (*moai*) to ancestors of high rank, and actually developed a written script to help them remember their chants and their royal family trees.

NEW ZEALAND

Far from the tropical lands of Melanesia and Micronesia and far from Hawaii and French Polynesia are the three islands of New Zealand. The *tangata whenua,* or first people of the land, were Polynesians.

According to old stories, the first explorer to reach New Zealand was a sea traveler called Kupe. This was perhaps a thousand years ago, a little before William the Conqueror invaded England.

When Kupe landed (say the legends), the country was so new it was drifting and trembling. The ground had not become hard enough to live on. One of the first things Kupe did was to make the land harden and stand still. Other tribal ancestors followed him in big canoes, or *whakas*. These were often double hulled like catamarans, with thatched awnings and sails. These later travelers brought plants such as *kumera* (a type of sweet potato), yams, and taros, and animals, too, so apparently when they set off, they expected to be at sea for a long time.

A STRANGE NEW COUNTRY

New Zealand was a lot colder than other Pacific islands. The *tangata whenua* had to wear new sorts of clothes and build warmer houses. They were used to wearing tapa cloth made from the bark of paper mulberry trees, but now tapa cloth was rare. Instead, the Maori plaited mats and clothes out of flax and the long, strong leaves of cabbage trees, while high-ranking warriors and chiefs wore cloaks of dogskin.

Though some of the food plants they had brought with them grew on the warmer North Island, they never grew quite as vigorously and easily in this cooler climate as they had on the islands closer to the equator. However, plants or no plants, the people had plenty to eat. The waters were full of fish. The Maoris were great fishermen, making fishhooks of bone and greenstone (a native jade), which were practical but also as beautiful as jewelry. Out of flax they made nets, sometimes very large ones, even hundreds of feet long, that would take several families to set and bring in. They also used eel pots and crayfish pots as well as hand lines. Family groups within the tribe would come together for fishing, and they fished most successfully, eating some of the fish fresh and drying and smoking the rest.

The forests of New Zealand were full of birds, including large ones that lived on the ground. Until the coming of men, there had been no predators. The ground was as safe for birds as the trees. Among the favorite food birds of the early Maori was the moa, one of the largest birds that has ever lived.

SETTLING IN

The first settlements were by river mouths or in bays and harbors. After all, the *tangata whenua* were used to the sea and wanted to live close to it and the food it supplied so generously. Partly because it was warmer, the Maoris tended to prefer the North Island to the South, and lived there as successful hunter-gatherers for many, many years.

During the fifteenth century things began to change. As an easy food bird, the moa had vanished from the bush. The Maori had killed it off. Even seals were not as plentiful as they had been in the beginning. Not only that, the human population was growing. So during the fifteenth century, the Maori became more dependent on planting and cultivating *kumera*. Consequently they became more dependent on village life. They changed from a society of hunters and gatherers to a society that relied on plants and crops. They did not stop hunting, of course. They still trapped pigeons; speared ground-dwelling birds like the kiwi and the weka, hunting them with dogs; and pulled young muttonbirds from their nest holes. They also ate the native rat, the *kiore,* they had brought with them.

However, in spite of the fishing and the hunting, *kumera* crops became more and more important to the Maori during the fifteenth century, and their way of life began to change. After the ground had been cleared and turned over with wooden digging sticks, the *kumera* were planted. Fences were put up to protect the delicate plants, which were tended by women until autumn and then dug up with ceremony, after which came a time of feasting.

When any people begin to grow things, they have to settle down and look after their land. They build villages, and because they do not have to carry things from place to place, they tend to gather more possessions together. And when people start to grow crops and gain possessions, they have to protect them, which means they become more warlike. During the fifteenth century, the Maori not only built villages, but fortified them with hidden trenches and high walls. Indeed, the villages needed to be defended, as villagers sometimes attacked each other, the defeated becoming slaves of the victors.

OPPOSITE: *Maori carved mask. Maori warriors wore facial tattoos with patterns very like the one in the mask here.*

VILLAGE LIFE

A Maori village, or *pa*, was made up of storehouses where food and treasures were kept and small houses with thickly thatched roofs and walls and porches in front. Each of these houses, which were tall enough for people to stand in, had a single small window. This allowed the escape of smoke from a fire in the center. However, Maori people used these houses differently from the way we use houses now. They slept in them on winter nights, but most of their living, their working and talking, was done out on the porch in front of the house. Maori people did not eat in their houses. That was *tapu*, or forbidden. They ate in the open or, in wet weather, on their porches. There were special shelters in which babies were born and where people were put when they were dying. The houses of tribal chiefs were small, too, but they were decorated with wonderful wood carvings, which became more elaborate and polished during the fifteenth century. The women did most of the village work, and the men, though they still hunted, had time to carve wood and greenstone. Often the figure of an ancestor would be part of the central pillar inside the house. In front of the chief's house was a special area of ceremonial land called the *marae*. Meetings were held and visiting tribes received there, and often there were great feasts.

Things changed for the Maori. Families and chiefs came and went. Some tribes grew powerful. Others weakened. Nevertheless the change was slow until the coming of the Europeans. Then things began to change very quickly indeed.

AUSTRALIA

Nobody really knows when the first people came to Australia. Certainly there have been people there so long that it seemed, to them at least, as if they must have been there forever. They felt they began there.

The first Australians probably came down through Indonesia during the Ice Age when more land was exposed. They found themselves in a country that was wetter and more fertile than it is today—a lonely land with long coastlines stretching from the warm, semitropical north to the cool, temperate south. Carbon

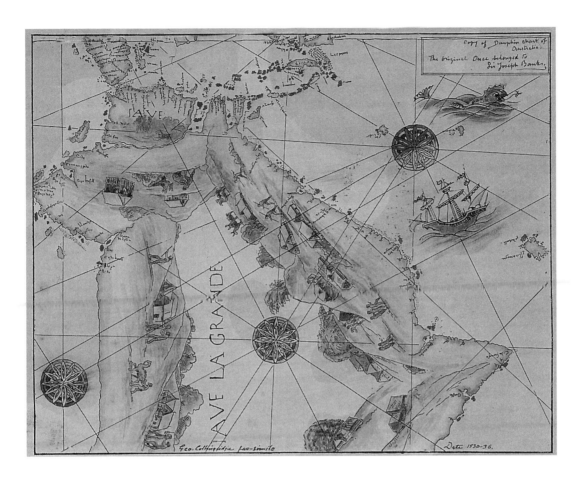

dating suggests that one skeleton found at Lake Mungo in Australia had been there for thirty-seven thousand years, and there are signs of older settlements still, though some experts disagree. However, we can be sure that whatever the correct dating, there have been people living in Australia for a very long time. When sea levels rose after the Ice Age, Australia became an isolated land.

The first Australians probably did not bring any sort of gardening skills with them, and even if they had, the plants and animals of this new country were not suitable for farming or gardening. The farms and market gardens of Australia today are filled with plants and animals that have been introduced from Europe, Asia, and the Americas.

Australia is an old country and its mammals are of an ancient kind known as marsupials. Their babies are born at an early stage of development and carried in pouches until they are old enough to set out on their own. In the beginning the Aborigines shared

Australia was unknown to Europe until the eighteenth century. But this 1536 Portuguese map may show the east coast of Australia. Compare the shape of the coastline lying to the left of the ship, to the shape of northern Australia in the map on page 99.

their country with the rhinoceroslike, plant-eating *diprotodon* (probably the biggest marsupial that ever lived) and the *procoptodon*, a giant kangaroo. There were giant tortoises and koalas and *thylacines*, meat-eating animals like the wolves of Tasmania. These were not true wolves but doglike marsupials. The Aborigines lived on what they could gather or kill from day to day. They were successful hunters and probably helped wipe out the diprotodon. This day-to-day hunting and gathering worked well. Aborigines were certainly well established by several thousand years ago, living mostly around the coasts or along the lines of rivers. Some tribes even learned to live in the desert interior.

THE DREAMTIME AND THE MAGICAL HOMELAND

When native Australians tell stories of their beginnings, they talk as if those beginnings were in Australia, whereas the Polynesians mostly tell tales of voyages from distant homelands and of the canoes they arrived in. For the Aboriginal people everything began with the Dreamtime, when the world was a great, limitless plain. Out of the plain rose the first spirits of the land, spirits of power shaped like kangaroos, snakes, and other animals, but with the minds of magical men and women. These spirits traveled across the plain, playing tricks on one another, until the time came for them to change. Then some of the first spirits rose into the sky and others sank down into the land, forming rocks and hills and rivers, becoming the landscape we recognize today. Among the animals that began to live in the hollows and holes and rivers of the land was man, man with his weapons, his laws, and his magical rituals.

A WONDERFUL ALLIANCE

The Aboriginal people adapted so well that when Europeans first arrived, they misunderstood the sort of life they saw. Aborigines did not need stone or wood houses as people in Europe did. They needed very few clothes. They made huts when necessary or slept in the open. They were not people who tried to own land or fence it in.

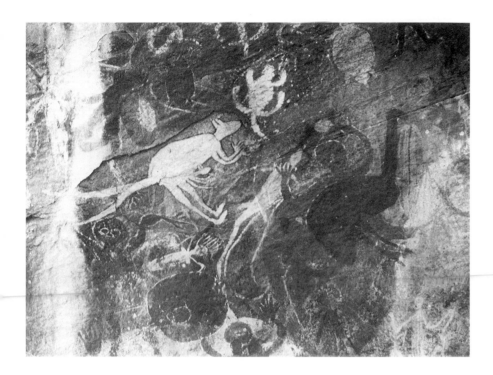

Aboriginal wall painting of a kangaroo, with joey in pocket.

They knew how to get water from plants. Certain plants such as the mallee and the mulga had water in their stems and roots. The kurrajong oak also held water. The water was vital. Water was life.

As well as watching for water, Aborigines hunted and gathered food. They had a variety of weapons that enabled them to kill animals, but much of their food was simply found in the land around them. They ate berries, leaves, and seeds. They also ate witchetty grubs (the larvae of a large moth), honey ants, and other insects, as well as frogs, lizards, tortoises, and snakes. As they marched through the day, the members of a family would keep a look out for anything tasty. When they camped, the men set off hunting big, flightless birds, such as the emu or the cassowary, or kangaroos and wombats. The women and children searched for small game. Hunters had various kinds of spears, some of which were hurled with a throwing stick, or *woomera*. They also had clubs like the *nulla nulla* and *waddy*. But their most famous weapon was the boomerang. Everybody knows that when a boomerang is thrown properly, it comes sweeping back to the thrower. However, these returning boomerangs were used most often in play. When Aborigine men hunted, they used a killing boomerang that did not return.

There was food in the water, too—shellfish, crabs, turtles, turtle eggs, seals, platypuses, even crocodiles, dugongs, and beached whales. The Aborigines speared fish or set traps for them, and sometimes made pools to keep fish alive until they were ready to be eaten.

FIRE

In the fifteenth century, Europeans were using tinder boxes to start fires; the Australians of the time made fire by rubbing hardwood sticks over softwood ones. This produced a smoldering wood powder that the fire maker then placed on dried grass. In south Australia fire makers used flints, which they struck against ironstone, producing sparks. Firesticks were carried from camp to camp. Samples taken from the floor of Lake George near Canberra show a dramatic increase in fires sometime between fifty thousand and a hundred thousand years ago—about the time humans first entered Australia.

Fire altered Australia. Some Australian trees—the eucalyptus, for example—actually need fire to germinate and grow. So when Aboriginal people brought fire to Australia, they encouraged the growth of those particular trees while eliminating many others. No other animal changes the world as quickly as human beings do. Like all people, the Aborigines used nature for their own purposes and changed the world around them.

FAMILY

Aboriginal people lived in tribes of as many as fifteen hundred people. However, these tribes had many smaller subgroups, each with a specific place in which to find food. An Aborigine child grew up as one of a band in which families would be closely related. Members of a band would probably have a Dreamtime ancestor in common, some bird or reptile or mammal. The family unit was very strong, and the rules that governed the family were strong too. Children were cherished, and adults would spend a lot of time playing with them, teaching them songs and games, and telling them stories. Children learned to wrestle, swim, and climb trees. As they mixed with adults, children learned to recognize birdsongs

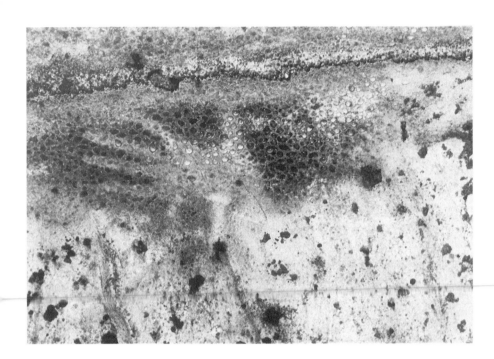

Thought to be between fifteen thousand and twenty thousand years old, this stenciled hand in a cave in Tasmania is among the oldest paintings in the world.

and the tracks of animals. They took on family responsibilities, learning to gather food and helping to support the group to which they belonged. The dingo, a species of dog, was domesticated, but dingoes were not working dogs. They seem to have been pets.

Like people everywhere, the Aborigines had their times of celebration and fun. A *corroberee* was a celebration filled with music and dancing. Connected to the celebrations was what we can only call a magical life affecting every member of the tribe, particularly the men.

Between the ages of thirteen and sixteen, boys would be initiated into the secrets of manhood. They were removed from normal camp life and taken to a place where the ceremonies could not be seen by women or by younger children. Preparation for these ceremonies sometimes took months. Decorated with ocher, a colored, earthy mixture used as a sort of yellowish-brown paint, and with human blood stuck with bird down, boys became men to the sound of ancient songs. Once they were initiated, they were expected to protect the secrets they had learned. The rituals that made up the ceremony were like plays. Hundreds of verses were memorized and in due course passed on to other young men. They danced to their songs and to the rhythm of stones and sticks slapped on the ground or against each other.

Girls were not a part of these secret rituals and ceremonies, though the women of some Aboriginal groups had songs and ceremonies of their own. Each girl had a husband chosen for her by a close male relative. From puberty on, a girl lived in the camp of her husband. Girls not only looked after children but, when the camp moved, carried babies, domestic articles, and containers of water. Men were not so heavily laden. They had to be free to hunt if necessary and perhaps to protect their band.

When Europeans came to Australia, they learned to respect the Aboriginal skills of observing nature and tracking and hunting. They made use of these skills when they needed to, but they did not understand Aboriginal culture, and the Aborigines did not understand the Europeans.

DISCOVERY

In many history books, the accounts of Australasia begin with what is called discovery. By *discovery* these historians do not mean the time that human beings first came to Australia or, later, to the far-flung islands. They mean the time that Europeans first landed on these distant shores, gave them new names, and described them as part of a "new world"—though of course these places were not new to the people already living there. They were as old as human memory itself. Histories often speak about the discovery of Australia and the islands as if the people already living there did not exist.

There have always been explorers, but Columbus was one of a group of adventurers who had the idea of finding wealth. These men wanted to satisfy curiosity, but they also wanted to grow rich. They set out first of all hoping to find new ways to old lands, imagining they might bring home precious stones, gold, and spices. They also wanted to spread word of Christianity. Having Christian faith themselves, explorers and men of the church wanted to convert the whole world. Some were quite sincere in this. Others used the idea to give some sort of dignity to their adventures and their greed.

Portugal and Spain, then France and England, sent out explorers with a generally more advanced technology than that of the peoples they encountered. But they also took a philosophy of life,

The so-called First Fleet arrives in Australia in 1788, bringing the continent's first European settlers.

an attitude toward land, that helped them succeed. They were brave and ruthless, and they believed (as most people seem to) that they were the *best* people, that their religion was the *right* religion, that other, different societies were inferior and did not deserve kindness or respect. This philosophy, together with their technological advantage, made them dangerous to whatever society they encountered. They were dangerous to the Aztecs and the Incas and other Native Americans. In due course they were dangerous to the peoples of Oceania, too.

Even the poorest and most ignorant European believed that he or she knew how land should be used, that the people of Australia and the Pacific islands were somehow wasting land because they did not mine it or farm it. The Europeans came and brought their families with them, and not only their families—they brought animals and plants, sometimes because they needed them to farm, sometimes because they liked these signs of home. Cats, dogs, rats, and weasels, along with the clearing of land, have almost wiped out New Zealand's ground-dwelling birds. Rabbits have reduced parts of New Zealand and Australia to desert.

In 1492 none of this was part of life for the people of Oceania, but it lay ahead of them. When Columbus set foot on San Salvador, ghosts of the future also began to stir on the shores of the Pacific islands.

THE AMERICAS IN 1492
Jamake Highwater

In the year Europeans call 1492, the land of the American Indians was already an ancient place. America had been discovered twenty-five to fifty thousand years earlier by small bands of people known as Paleo-Indians—nomadic hunters from the arctic regions of Asia who made their precarious way into the vast Western Hemisphere, where no human being had ever ventured. That land is now named North and South America. But long ago, when the ancient Indians made their miraculous journey into a truly new world, a great climatic crisis had overcome the earth: the temperature had plunged, and the polar seas froze into vast ice floes and glaciers. Sea levels dropped over three hundred feet, exposing a great, barren land bridge a thousand miles wide spanning the Bering Straits, the ice-bound region that now separates northeastern Asia from Alaska.

After the arrival of the Paleo-Indians, a great river of time swept across the Americas. The primitive hunters who discovered the Western Hemisphere transformed the continents of North and South America into their own world, a place unknown and unvisited by anyone else for countless centuries.

American Indians soon inhabited the entire Western Hemisphere from Alaska to Tierra del Fuego, the southernmost tip of South America—a distance of more than ten thousand miles. They conquered the longest new frontier in history, and the smoke of their countless campfires rose into the immense sky that shelters the two continents. Not until we reach another planet will we again explore so vast a domain.

By the year known as 1492, the first Americans had become greatly diversified in the way they looked and the way they lived. They spoke a great many languages, some as dissimilar to others as German is to Chinese. America produced a long succession of intricate cultures and brilliant civilizations. In 1492, many of the grandest of these American nations had already vanished into oblivion, leaving grand ruins as the only testament to their exis-

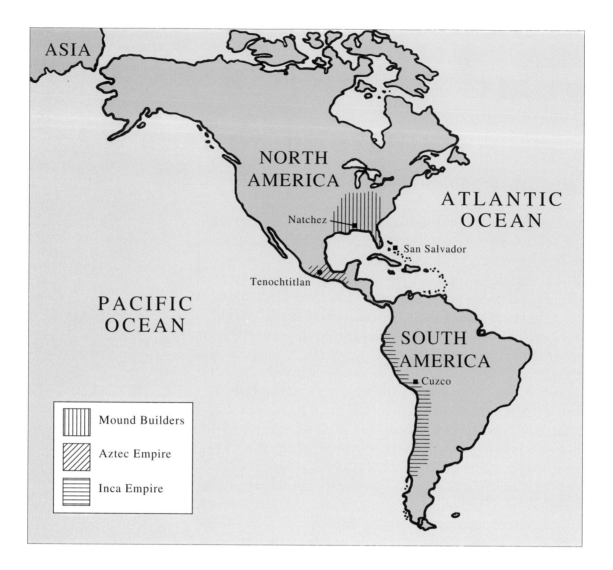

tence. The architects of these lost worlds were among the first great tribes of the Americas: the Olmecs, who were the mysterious originators of Mesoamerican culture; the astounding Maya, who brought American society to its grandest moment; the peaceful people of Teotihuacán; and the mighty Toltec warriors of central Mexico. Other Indian civilizations, such as the Aztecs of Mexico and the Incas of Peru, were at their highest glory in 1492, while still others were just beginning.

THE AZTECS

The Aztecs, who created a vast empire in the heart of the Valley of Mexico, were among the newly evolving nations. They called themselves the People of the Sun. And they told a sacred story about their origins in a mysterious homeland in northern Mexico.

The People of the Sun heard the voice of a bird that spoke to them from a tree, saying: "*Tihui . . . Let us go. I will call you Mexica and I will lead you to a promised land where you will be great among all the tribes.*"

The Mexica left their land in the desolate place north of the Colorado River and followed the voice of the bird, taking up their tribal god Huitzilopochtli and carrying him on a throne of rushes into the wilderness in search of a new homeland.

Their god said to them: "I shall lead you to the place you seek. There you shall build a temple which will be my house, my bed of grass. And in that same place you shall make your homes. And you shall conquer and rule all the land. And your mighty city shall be called Tenochtitlán, and you shall be the People of the Sun."

This ancient tale of the search for a homeland comes from the folk history of the Aztec (or Mexica) people. The story is an account of some actual events that took place in the years between 1160 and 1325, when the once humble Aztecs founded the last of several powerful empires that ruled the vast Mexican territories in North and Central America.

Standing at the center of this mighty domain was the imperial city, Tenochtitlán. Among the grand temples and pyramids of this great Mexican city, more than three hundred thousand people made their way along broad streets and avenues lined with sixty thousand houses. In 1492 this lavish Mexican capital was five times bigger than the city the European invaders called London. It had vastly superior plumbing, a far greater and more varied agricultural harvest, overwhelming wealth, and far less poverty and disease. Taking full advantage of the great legacy of the lost civilizations that both outshone and greatly predated them in the Valley of Mexico, the Aztecs borrowed other people's religions; they claimed other nations' histories; and they imitated the masterful arts and philosophies that originated among long-vanished nations such as the Olmecs, the Toltecs, and the Maya. They took over the cultures of the peoples they overran, and they rewrote history in order to make themselves the heroes of other people's sacred stories.

Poems in Nahuatl, the language of the Aztecs, recall a land on the eastern sea that was settled so long ago that "no one can

The Aztec god of war, Huitzilopochtli.

remember its history." Its name, Tamoanchan, is not from the Nahuatl but from the Maya and means Land of Rain—an apt description of the tropical rain forests of the Mexican Gulf Coast, where the Olmecs ascended to civilization during the first century B.C. The name Olmec comes from the language of the Aztecs, meaning "the rubber people," so named, apparently, because of the characteristic rubber ball they used in a ritual game. Very little is known about the ceremony except that it was a very serious game of life and death, played in a two-sided court with goal hoops on the elaborate stone walls. This game was probably invented in about 800 B.C. by the Olmecs, the most ancient of

The Mesoamerican ball game, as depicted on a Mayan vase from around the eighth century A.D. The ball itself is shown out of proportion here; it was actually about the size of a softball.

Mexico's peoples, and it spread, like many other aspects of Olmec life, throughout Mexico and then northward to the American Southwest and southward into Central America. Clearly, Olmec culture was very important to the development of civilization in the Americas. For instance, the Olmecs created the first masonry architecture in the Americas, the first written language, and the whole basis of Mexican religious life. Besides their invention of highly advanced agriculture and horticulture, they also possessed good pottery and excellent cotton cloth. From Olmec culture came the important gods as well as the religion, science, and astronomy of all later Mexican nations.

A key element in all of these societies was a philosophy that gave some people far greater power than others and that put an emphasis upon social rank and privilege. This philosophy justified the efforts of missionaries who were sent into every territory to convert people to the Mexican way of life. Another element of many Mexican religions was the practice of blood sacrifice, which was widespread in Middle America.

Another highly religious people who had a great impact on the world of the Aztecs were the ancient Maya. Behind every religious act of the Maya were the mystic dictates of their calendar, for the Maya were absolutely obsessed with time.

To devise their complex calendars, the Maya had to be great mathematicians. A very important achievement in their thinking was the invention of zero, an abstract concept essential to all advanced calculations, which was discovered by only two other peoples in world history: the Babylonians and the Hindus. Even the Greeks and the Romans, at the height of their civilizations, had no concept of zero, and it was not introduced into Europe until the Middle Ages.

Using their characteristic military abilities and shrewdness, the Aztecs began to insinuate themselves into the Mexican tribes that surrounded them, becoming mercenaries—paid soldiers—of the powerful Tepanec nation, ruled by a chief called Tezozomoc. As the various city-states of the Valley of Mexico fell to Lord Tezozomoc and his allies, the Aztecs not only shared in the booty, but

The Aztec calendar combined a ritual period of 260 days with a civic period of 365 days. Every fifty-two years, the two periods coincided and completed a cycle.

A priest tears the hearts out of sacrificial victims on the steps of a temple in this picture from an Aztec codex.

they were also taken under the protection of the Tepanecs. They learned much from their Tepanec allies, particularly the arts of military expansion, statecraft, and empire building. After generations of humiliation, the Aztecs were now ready to become a singular and dominant force in Mexico. Their opportunity came in 1426, when the Tepanec king Tezozomoc was succeeded by his son Maxtlatzin, who wished to do away with the Aztecs because of their ever-growing political power. This plan to subdue the Aztecs came precisely when a new and remarkable king was elected to the Aztec throne. His name was Itzcoatl, and he was determined and ruthless. He decided to fight the Tepanecs rather than allow his people to be crushed by their young king.

Within two years the Aztec Lord Itzcoatl had defeated the

Tepanecs and destroyed their city. This decisive victory made the Aztecs the greatest power in Mexico. It took many human sacrifices to maintain such a position of greatness. According to Aztec religious mythology, their tribal god Huitzilopochtli, represented by the sun, was required each day to fight a heroic battle against the powers of darkness in order to be reborn into the eastern sky each dawn. This fierce deity demanded human hearts and human blood in order to strengthen himself for his daily ordeal. Human sacrifice therefore became a major element of Aztec ritual. To keep political control of Mexico, but also to make captives available for sacrifice, the Aztecs devised a curious form of warfare, called the Flowery Wars, a series of attacks on various neighboring allies. One purpose of these wars was to capture foreign soldiers for sacrifice. The Flowery Wars also provided the opportunity for the assassination of enemy rulers, bountiful plunder, the acquisition of slaves, and the constant expansion of Aztec territory. Warfare had always been attractive to many of the civilizations of Mexico. It was the Aztecs, however, who elevated war to the state of religious celebration.

The greatest empire-builder and perhaps the bloodiest of all the Aztec rulers was Lord Ahuitzotl, who ruled from 1486 to 1502. Ahuitzotl subjugated all the nations as far south as the Guatemalan border and brought almost all of central Mexico under Aztec command. A pitiless man of immense militaristic ambition and unlimited energy, Ahuitzotl ordered the completion of the Great Temple of Tenochtitlán, which had been under construction for many years before his reign. For the dedication of that massive temple in 1487, he had twenty thousand people sacrificed.

The most tragic and illustrious of the mighty Aztec lords was Lord Montezuma Xocoyotzin. Unlike his bloodthirsty predecessors on the Aztec throne, Montezuma was a philosophical king. Ironically, it was his meditative nature and profound interest in the artistic and spiritual heritage of the ancient Toltecs that destroyed him and ultimately brought down the entire Aztec world. When he heard the startling news that a small band of strangers had landed on the shores of Mexico, every decision Montezuma made was the result of his devout belief in Toltec legends that foretold that he would preside over the total destruction of Mexican civilization. He did not defend himself against his foreign kidnappers and assassins, and he refused to send his thousands upon thousands of expert soldiers against the mere six hundred intruders, whom he believed to be ancient Mexican gods returning to take command of their rightful kingdom.

Montezuma's capital was one of the great cities of the world. On market day, the crowds were large and noisy. Humble and great persons hurried in every direction, the rich carrying flowers, which only they were allowed to possess, while the poor carried their heavy burdens. In a small ball court, with its sloping masonry sides and narrow playing field, a few men were practicing the game called *pot-a-tok*. The expression of the young athletes was grim as they raced after the hard rubber ball and, using their heads, their thighs, and their feet, tried to keep it from striking the floor of the ball court. For the Aztecs, it was a sport of great daring and deep religious significance.

The Aztec day began when the priests at the top of the great pyramids beat wooden gongs and sounded trumpets made of conch seashells. It was still dawn as the people awakened in all the houses, great and humble. Most of the homes were made of sun-

For amusement, the Aztecs played games of chance. The one pictured in this codex was similar to the Hindu game of pachisi.

baked bricks and consisted of one large family room, with the kitchen located in a separate building in the courtyard. In the first light of the day, the women fanned the coals of their cooking fires until they burst into flame. In the gardens turkeys began to strut and gobble, while in the houses there was the rumble of corn grinders. Soon there was also the rhythmic sound of the women slapping lumps of dough between their hands to make the pancake-like bread called *tlaxcalli* (or tortillas). Now all the families came together to have breakfast, a simple meal of bread and a beer-like drink called *octli*. Then, after a bath in fresh water, using a soap made from the root of the *copalxocotl* tree, they put on their sandals and tied their cloth cloaks over their shoulders and were ready for work.

Outside the city, most people worked in the fields from dawn to dusk. For their long day they packed a picnic lunch, which they called *itacatl,* and then they went into the fields owned by their town or village. They grew corn, vegetables, and flowers, for which the Aztecs had a great affection. All Mexicans shared this love of gardens. The people grew flowers everywhere—in their courtyards, in broad fields along the lakes, and even on their rooftops. Many families also had household pets: rabbits, turkeys, dogs, bees, and often parrots and macaws.

The main meal of the day was in the early afternoon, when the

The Aztecs grew maize, tomatoes, chocolate, black beans, pumpkins, and avocados as well as many other fruits and vegetables. This codex page shows some of the Aztecs' foodstuffs.

OPPOSITE: *Ceremonial mask made of turquoise and shell. The face is formed by two intertwining serpents.*

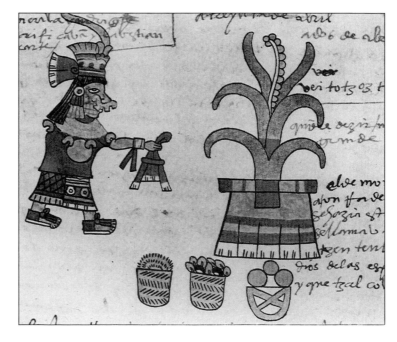

sun was so hot that the people sought the shelter of shady trees. For field workers, this meal consisted of cornbread, beans, a sauce made of pimientos and tomatoes, chili cakes called tamales, and, on special occasions, game meat such as venison (deer) or poultry (turkey). The families sat on the ground on mats, sharing each dish and talking about the day's work. These simple people knew very little about the great city of Mexico. For them, Montezuma, the mighty ruler of the Aztec world, was a god, as distant as the moon. The common people could not read the signs in the heavens, the messages of the stars. Only the priests could read them and learn the future. The people could not understand the books, called codices, in which scholars drew elaborate pictures of events of the

A 1556 Italian map of Mexico City (Tenochtitlán), based on sketches made by the first Conquistadors.

past and present as their way of keeping history. The Aztecs had neither invented a written language nor inherited the written language of the Maya.

The common people of Mexico were born, they worked, and then they died. They had little opportunity for education or advancement. During the first years of their lives, boys were taught to carry wood and water. By the age of six, girls learned how to spin cloth and to cook. At the age of fifteen, young people who showed signs of intelligence and talent were allowed to enter the *calmecac*—a temple school where their education was entrusted to priests.

For the Aztec people of wealth and power, life was very different from the existence of the farmers and their families. They had lavish food and educational opportunities. They lived in the great city among the splendid temples and pyramids, and they wandered among the magnificent buildings and gardens as free people.

In the main plaza at the heart of the royal city of Tenochtitlán, there was a great sea of human bodies and human baggage. Then, quite suddenly, the tangle of the crowd opened into the vast empty space at the entrance to the palace. Only men of power and rank were allowed to walk in this expansive entranceway. One by one they came to the Council Chamber of Montezuma to plead for favors or to beg forgiveness for an offense. He was more than a ruler. He was very nearly a god—so great and so holy that no one was allowed to look upon his face. He was elected from the most royal of Aztec lineages by a council of nobles, warriors, and high priests. But once he ascended to the throne, he was utterly out of reach even to those who had elected him, so vast was his power. Great lords were required to wear the plainest garments in his presence. They spoke to him only indirectly, through an "interpreter." Wherever Lord Montezuma went, he was carried on a litter perched on the shoulders of nobles, and wherever he walked the ground was swept and covered with precious textiles. Even when he dined, Montezuma was concealed behind a handsome screen, lest anyone see so holy a person engaging in a mortal act like eating.

To the Aztec people, Montezuma was the greatest ruler of the world. Yet even as Montezuma dined in solitude in his magnificent palace, there lived another great Indian king of whom Montezuma and his people had no knowledge.

THE INCAS

A decade after the death of Montezuma, in the thin, mountainous air of the high Andes of South America, a few thousand miles to the south of Mexico, the Inca Lord Atahualpa sat at his magnificent supper. To the people of his empire he was the greatest ruler in the world. He was the Sun King of Peru, the Sapa Inca, owner of all that existed. As Inca legends proclaim: "All that lay under the sun was his."

If Montezuma was almost divine, Atahualpa was truly a god, descended directly from the Great Sun, the creator of the land and the people and all that was precious upon the earth. For the Incas, gold was the sweat of Father Sun and silver was the tears of Mother Moon. Atahualpa owned all the glistening gifts of these heavenly beings. His power was absolute. There were no checks or balances; there was no Inca court of appeal. Lord Atahualpa was a ruler of almost unlimited power. Only the possibility of revolt among his people, if they became dissatisfied with his behavior, cautioned him. With only a gesture of his hand, Atahualpa, the Sapa Inca, could order the death of a great warrior or even a royal relative. Yet despite the extent of power of Inca rulers, there was much reason to admire their concern for the people. This charity was largely the result of an extraordinary form of government unique to the Inca Empire. The land was owned by the state. A citizen had only the use of the land. Yet people were not slaves, and they were free to accumulate personal wealth and luxuries.

The government took care of its citizens. They were protected from want and from civil unrest and crimes against themselves and their families. Great storehouses were maintained, and the supplies were used to feed the people in times of famine. For these privileges the Incas paid heavy taxes in the form of both produce and labor.

The success of the Inca Empire was based on its ability to produce ample supplies not only for its religious leaders, armies, and ranking aristocrats, but also for all people, noble and peasant alike. Every aspect of life was controlled by the unshakable, supreme authority of their ruler and god, the Sapa Inca. On behalf of the Sapa Inca, state officials traveled among the villages to arrange marriages. Such officials also determined the amount of produce each village was required to give to the state, and they assigned

The Incas carved terraces into steep mountainsides in order to increase the amount of useful land. Shown here are the ruins of the last Inca city, Machu Picchu.

military and labor service to adult men. The Inca rulers inherited from their royal forebears the unshakable authority that in Europe was called the divine right of kings—the notion that the authority of monarchs cannot be questioned because it is given to them by God. There has never been a social organization quite like the Inca Empire.

The empire was based on the control of food supplies. Such great stocks of materials required a system of careful bookkeeping. Although the Incas, like the Aztecs in the north, did not have a written language, they did use a special device, called a *quipu*, for keeping accounts. It consisted of an elaborate arrangement of strings hung in a series on a master cord. The strings were dyed a multitude of colors, and each string held knots along its length. The styles, sizes, colors, and locations of the knots signified com-

modities, persons, accounts, and various numbers and amounts. Though *quipus* from the time of the Incas still exist, the secret of reading them has been lost.

The architecture of the Incas was brilliant, created entirely of huge, meticulously fitted stones interlocked with one another without the use of mortar or cement. Architects conceived the Inca capital, Cuzco, in the form of a crouching puma—an American mountain lion. In the west of the city was the great plaza where the common people gathered to celebrate their festivals. In the east was the plaza that was the civic center of Cuzco and from which spread the four districts of the city, divided into twelve communities. At its height, in 1492, Cuzco was crowded with people from every part of the realm, all dressed in their traditional costumes, proudly individual in their tribal customs while at the same time strongly devoted to the powerful empire that unified them.

For the common people, the day began when Father Sun climbed into the sky. Their breakfast was simple: a drink of *aka,* a slightly fermented, thick beverage. Then they went to the fields to work, for most of the inhabitants of the empire were farmers. The empire had taught them that working the land was a divine undertaking and a form of worship. The midday meal brought together the extended family of children, mother, father, grandparents, and other relatives. The food consisted of a dish called *mote*—made of corn, chili peppers, and herbs, boiled or baked in hot ashes. A major source of meat was a small creature that freely scampered about the dwellings: guinea pigs, called *cui*.

The midday meal was served on a cloth spread on the ground, with the men crouched around the pots of food. The women sat outside the circle, their backs turned toward the men. All the family members helped themselves to the food, using their fingers or drinking broth from ceramic bowls. Conversation was quiet but pleasant, although there was little exchange between the men and the women. After the meal, the people returned to the fields.

The tropical evening came quickly in the high Andes, and soon the door-flaps of the houses were lowered, and families went inside and hovered around their fires. The young listened as the elders recited tales of gods and battles and ancestors. The women ground corn and made cloth from the hair of two unique Andean mammals, the llama and the alpaca.

The education of the young was an imitation of their parents'

OPPOSITE: *The Incas were skilled artists, as this vibrant puma head testifies.*

daily lives. At fourteen most boys put on breechclouts and took their permanent names, either that of an uncle or of their father. It was a very different matter for the son of a noble family. For him, reaching maturity involved a pilgrimage to the birthplace of the Inca Empire at Huanacauri, located far up the Cuzco Valley.

Young women celebrated reaching maturity with a hair-combing ceremony and a new name derived from the stars or a plant.

Out of such a unique social structure, the Incas created a world not unlike the Roman Empire. The city of Cuzco was their Rome. From this wondrous city the Inca lords planned and achieved the domination of a realm larger than anything that had come before it in South America. But also like the Romans, the Incas created almost nothing that was truly new. Both Rome and Cuzco excelled

An Inca quipu keeper. From a sixteenth-century drawing.

in engineering, military exploitation, and social administration. Just as the Romans borrowed most of the elements of the civilization from Egypt and Greece, and just as the Aztecs borrowed their culture from the Olmecs, Maya, and Toltecs, so too the Incas derived most of their culture from several long-lost civilizations of the Andes, known today only through their astonishing works of art. Even the Inca language, which the Inca lords imposed upon every tribe they conquered as a means of unifying the empire, seems to have been appropriated from another, more ancient culture that originated in northern Peru. Nonetheless, the Incas possessed great genius of their own: a remarkable capacity for social organization and administration in war and in peace.

Peace prevailed among tribes that had persistently fought one another before the domination of the Inca Empire. The sons of subdued chieftains were taken to the royal court in the great city of Cuzco. There they remained as honored guests—though, in truth, they were actually hostages who guaranteed the good behavior of their communities. The idols representing the gods of various tribes were also taken hostage and kept in Cuzco. If, despite such precautions, there was civil disorder within a particular tribe, the Inca authorities moved the troublemakers to another, more loyal community. An equal number of good citizens, called *mitmaes*, were sent to live with the troublesome tribe.

Despite such political techniques, there was always some sort of civil strife among the Inca tribes. These revolts were quickly and fiercely suppressed. When the Canari people of southern Ecuador rebelled against the Inca Lord Atahualpa, he had all the men of the tribe exterminated at the place thereafter called Yaguarcocha—"The Lake of Blood."

On the whole, however, the success of Inca imperialism was impressive. By the year 1492, the empire, called Tawantinsuyu, "The Four Quarters of the World," was a huge realm occupying most of the Pacific coast of South America. The Incas were now in total control of Ecuador and Peru, and their armies were battling as far north as Colombia, where they were trying in vain to subdue several highly independent provinces. Had they had more time, they surely would have battled their way as far north as the Caribbean. But their world ended abruptly when Atahualpa received the terrible news that white men who looked like demons had come from the sea and were marching upon his great empire.

THE MOUND BUILDERS

The influence of Mexican and Andean civilizations was felt, directly or indirectly, in virtually every region of the Americas. In the Southwest of what is now the United States, a series of villages greatly influenced by Mexican culture had existed for centuries, beginning with the vanished Anazasi, Hohokam, and Mimbres peoples and ending with the Pueblo Indians who now inhabit New Mexico and Arizona. But none of the nations that fell under the spell the Mexican and Andean empire-builders were as bizarre and mysterious as the North American societies called Mound Builders, named for the massive mounds of earth that they made along river valleys. We know nothing about the languages or the origins of these people. We know only that they were a very complicated group of tribal communities, that they constructed great mounds of dirt, or earthworks, and that they produced masterful works of art before declining and vanishing. One thing we do know for certain, these master builders of earthworks along the great rivers of North America were some of the Americas' most extraordinary inhabitants.

The Mound Builders were not one society but a long succession of tribes. They lived under the control of unbelievably powerful chiefs, who directed the construction of earthen mounds and the establishment of countless settlements along the Ohio and Mississippi rivers. Thousands of earthworks dot an extensive territory reaching all the way from Florida to Canada. The geographical range of Mound Builder culture is truly spectacular.

The story of the Mound Builders begins about three thousand years ago, shortly after the introduction of agriculture in the eastern region of the United States. At about this time the hunters of the area gradually settled in large villages, where they began to produce crude pottery. By about 1550 B.C., they had begun to raise crops such as corn, squash, and beans. About 1000 B.C., the first primitive mounds were under construction. Some mounds were used as burial sites, while others were apparently designed as forts. Still others, like the immense mounds in the shape of birds and serpents, had ceremonial purposes. It is also likely that wooden temples and official buildings and noble homes were constructed on at least some of the mounds.

An almost unbelievable amount of effort and dedication was

needed to build the mounds. For instance, a huge mound near St. Louis covers fifteen acres and is one hundred feet high. It contains more than twenty-two million cubic feet of earth. All that dirt was carried by hand, one basketful at a time, by a large population of dedicated or driven people who did their difficult work entirely without beasts of burden or wheeled vehicles.

In the year 1492 the cultural traditions of the ancient Mound Builders were still alive among a series of small, riverside states on the lower Mississippi. One of these states belonged to about seven thousand Natchez Indians, whose villages were scattered along what is now called St. Catherines Creek. The Natchez were ruled by a chief, the Great Sun, whose power was virtually unlimited. Like the lord of the Incas, the Natchez chief owned all the land

A mound in the shape of a serpent, in Ohio. The coiled tail is at the left; the head appears to be swallowing an egg.

and all the personal property, and the lives of his subjects were totally in his control. His house, constructed of timber, was positioned on the top of a flat mound. A second mound was the location of a wooden temple in which the bones of deceased Great Suns were kept. The relatives of the Great Sun were called Little Suns, and they were respected in accordance with their blood relationship to the Great Sun himself. All the Suns, Great and Little, had many voluntary servants who hunted and worked for them without reward.

Below the Great Sun and his immediate family was a rigidly graded aristocracy, consisting of nobles, and then war chiefs, high priests, and, finally, the lowest-ranking of the aristocrats, the Honored Men or Honored Women, including master artisans, rich merchants, and important soldiers.

The commoners, consisting of farmers, workers, warriors, and slaves, were all called Stinkards, or Stinkers—a massive population

This beautifully carved wooden head of a deer was found in an ancient Mound Builder site in present-day Florida.

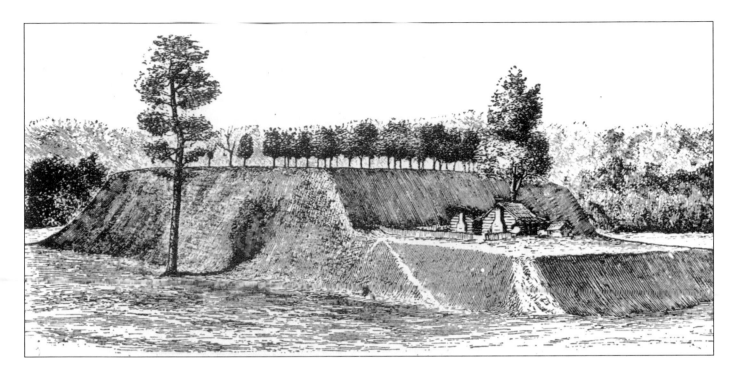

Some mounds were built upon by later European settlers, as in this log-cabin homestead in Arkansas.

without any voice in the running of their world or their own lives. They were killed at whim, should their actions or comments displease the Great Sun or his court. Their social situation might have been utterly hopeless were it not for one curious rule of Natchez life: all aristocrats, including the Great Sun himself, were required to marry Stinkers. This marital arrangement did not relieve commoners of their wretched situation, but on the other hand, the children of such a union were permitted to rise in rank, depending on the station of the mother. Thus an offspring of a noble mother and her Stinker husband became a noble. But the child of a noble father and a Stinker mother assumed the next rank below that of the father, becoming an Honored Man or Honored Woman. The son of the Great Sun could not inherit his father's supreme rank; instead, the Great Sun was succeeded when he died by the son of his highest-ranking female relative. The fact that social rank came from mothers instead of fathers resulted in a respected role in the life of the tribe for Natchez women. For instance, only the Stinker wife of the Great Sun had the right to eat at his table. The other members of his family, the so-called Little Suns, were given the leftovers from the Great Sun's table, which he offered to them by pushing the food toward them with his foot. The daughters of noble families had to marry Stinkers, but they had the right to turn their Stinker husbands away when they pleased and to take another husband. The Stinker husband of a noble woman had to stand in her presence, he could not eat with her, and he had to salute her in the same manner used by slaves. The only privilege of the Stinker husband was that he did not have to work.

Marriage was not an important part of Natchez life, except for its relationship to social rank. On the other hand, death and the funeral rites associated with death were regarded with the greatest attention. Every detail of the death and burial of the Great Sun was a matter of custom and law. When the Great Sun died, his wife began to weep, throwing back her head and howling a death cry. The sound was taken up by all the attendants and relatives of the ruler, until the entire village resounded with the lamentation. For two days elaborate preparations for the funeral were made. The Great Sun lay in state, adorned in his finest costume, his face painted red. By his side were the emblems of his power: a war club, numerous stone pipes, his bow and arrow, and a chain of cane woven with a succession of links, each representing an enemy he had killed in battle.

At a signal from the high priest, the attendants lifted the litter of the dead king and a solemn procession began. It made its way down the stately mound on which the Great Sun's house was perched and slowly wound into the plaza. Then the litter bearing the dead man was carried toward the temple mound that flanked the plaza. A group of women raised their voices in the sad chant of death as the procession started the climb to the temple at the top of the mound. The howls rose louder, and to the accompaniment of this immense lamentation, the body of the Great Sun was carried to the summit of the burial mound and placed in a grave along with offerings of fine ornaments, weapons, and pottery. Slowly the grave was filled, while on the mound across the village, where the Great Sun had once lived, a great cloud of smoke rose as the royal house was burned to the ground.

THE PLAINS INDIANS

The smoke was caught by a swift wind that carried it high into the sky arching over America, stretching westward across woodlands

and lakes and the Great Plains that sprawled between Texas and Canada and between the Mississippi River and the Rocky Mountains, filling an unbroken landscape with a sea of grass. The Indian people of the Great Plains knew little of the Mound Builders except for the rare objects they sent to them by way of their trade routes. These Plains Indians did not create great temples and villages. Instead they were nomads and hunters who believed that every element of the land was alive and sacred. Their world was a world of grass. The great prairie of 1492 was a desolate place where few people lived. In those days there was not a single horse in all the Americas, nor any other animal on which Indian hunters could thunder across the grasslands in pursuit of the swift and burly buffalo. The only beast of burden of the Plains Indian was the dog, which dragged the belongings of small bands of nomads

Bison skin, painted by a Navajo artist soon after the introduction of the horse to the Americas.

as they traveled from place to place, supporting themselves by gathering wild plants and hunting on foot. Theirs was a highly individual world, unconcerned with appointing high priests or producing temples and cities. The religious life of the Plains was largely in the hands of the individual, who had personal chants and personal sacred objects and sacred drawings, often discovered in dreams or handed down from one generation to the next. In the summer, during the time of the hunt, the people gathered into large bands and lived in portable tents called tipis. They tracked animal herds over long distances and were constantly on the move. In the winter, much smaller groups settled by themselves in isolated areas. In these cold months, Plains Indians took shelter in earthen pit-houses (or lodges) built near streams and rivers. They lived on dried meat, fruits, and whatever fresh prey was available. They stayed close to home, and at night, under the beadwork of the sky, they told stories about their adventures and exploits as the smoke of their campfires rose into the starry heavens.

SAN SALVADOR

Again the smoke is caught by a swift wind, which carries it high into the broad sky that arches over America, stretching across woodlands and lakes and the wide plains, and beyond the mouth of the great river that pours its muddy water into the warm waters of the Gulf of Mexico.

There, among the tropical islands of the Caribbean, suddenly the smoke vanishes into a gray morning.

On that morning of October 12, 1492, a miraculous sight is seen by the people of a little island, now called High Cay, that lies just off the coast of San Salvador in the Caribbean Sea. There in the twilight, as they climb from their hammocks and come out of their palm-leaf-covered houses, they see three moving islands that gradually make their way across the water, coming out of the great unknown and moving ever closer to the astonished people on the shore. In the first light, the floating islands give birth to small rafts that float away from their mothers and drift toward the beach, carrying the most unbelievable of creatures. They look like people made of bright colors. Their faces are covered with bushy hair, as if they are holding squirrels in their mouths.

Despite the strangeness of these creatures, the people are delighted and astounded to see them, and they run toward the water to greet them. At close range, the people realize that the strangers from the sea look like real men, except they have very pale faces covered with bunches of curly hair. They are terribly ugly and have a dreadful smell of spoiled milk. Yet they seem harmless, despite the strange gray and black weapons they carry. The people smile happily when the strangers admire their spears made of reeds and the lovely little ornaments of gold they wear on their ears and nostrils. The people cannot understand why the yellow metal is so fascinating to them. To make them happy, they bring their strange guests many gifts—green parrots and bundles of precious cotton— in return for which they are given beautiful colored beads and small bells that make a delightful sound. These strangers, who completely hide themselves behind clothing, seem ill at ease with the nakedness of the people of the island, who do not cover their handsome bodies except for lavish painted designs of black, white, and red.

Then a man with a scarlet chest steps forward and tries to talk to the people, though he does not know how to speak properly and can only make strange noises and wave his arms in the air. Despite this strange behavior, the people smile at him respectfully. Hoping to teach him how to speak, they gesture across the landscape, and they tell the scarlet man that their island is called Guanahani. He seems to understand. Then the man points to himself and repeatedly tells the people his name. At this the people of the island begin to laugh. For this stranger has a most peculiar name!

Christopher Columbus.

NOTES

Europe

page 2 Jerusalem is considered the Holy City by Christians, Jews, and Muslims. It was the site of Solomon's temple and also the site of the Church of the Resurrection, supposedly situated on the spot of Jesus' tomb. Since Muslims believed that their founder, Muhammad, also visited Jerusalem, the city is holy to them too. When the Muslims first captured Jerusalem in 627, they did not harm the holy places of the Christians. But in 1010 a Muslim ruler, Hakim, was less tolerant. He destroyed the Church of the Resurrection (also called the Church of the Holy Sepulcher), and this led to the First Crusade (1095–99).

page 10 Saunas were also popular in the Scandinavian countries.

Forks were used first in the fifteenth century in Italy, but they were not common. Even a century later the English made fun of forks as a foreign fad. Some even disapproved. If God had meant people to use forks, they said, He wouldn't have given them fingers.

page 13 Moscow was founded in 1156, when Yur Dolgoruki built a wall around his villa, which made it look like a fortress (*kreml*). Later the enclosure was enlarged, and churches and palaces were built within what is now known as the Kremlin. Ivan III reconstructed it. He was the first Russian ruler to call himself a czar (a shortened form of "caesar").

The Russian Orthodox Church was once part of the Greek Catholic Church, but it had become independent, renouncing any allegiance to a pope.

page 15 Johannes Gutenberg was born about 1400. His father's name was Gensfleish, or Gooseflesh, but he didn't care for the name, so he used his mother's maiden name. His first type-printed book appeared in 1456 or 1457 and is known now as the Gutenberg Bible. Although printing spread quickly, some people called it a vulgar invention. What would happen to the art of manuscript writing? they asked. What would happen to the beautiful manuscript libraries?

page 21 Michelangelo Buonarroti, 1475–1564. He is perhaps most famous for his painting of the ceiling of the Sistine Chapel, which took him from 1508 to 1512 to complete.

Leonardo da Vinci, 1452–1519. One of his most famous paintings is the *Mona Lisa*.

Asia

page 34 In Mongolian, the word for camp (each tribe had its own camp) is *ordu,* from which we get the English word "horde."

page 35 You can still read Marco Polo's book. Look in your library for *The Travels of Marco Polo.*

page 36 An even more terrible event delayed the development of European culture. In the middle of the fourteenth century, a scourge of bubonic plague known as the Black Death killed twenty-five million people, or almost half of Europe's population. It seems to have originated in China and was carried like other items of trade by the fleas on rats, which were common stowaways on merchant ships. The plague threw Europe into social and economic chaos. The Doge was the elected chief magistrate of the city-state of Venice.

page 38 The Muslim scripture, the Koran, is unlike the scriptures of Judaism and Christianity. The Bible is a collection of books written by a great variety of writers over a long span of time, perhaps more than a thousand years. The Koran is a single book written about the life and teachings of Muhammad, the prophet and founder of Islam. It is thought to be the work of a single writer and written close to the prophet's own time (A.D. 570–632). Islam (the word means "obedience" or "submission to the word of God") came out of a culture where many gods were worshiped. Muhammad declared that there was only one God, Allah the Beneficent and Merciful. Ask your librarian for more information about Muhammad and the faith of Islam.

page 45 A eunuch is a man who has been castrated. In ancient times eunuchs were valued as guards for a ruler's harems. They served as court officials and often rose to positions of power and trust.

A *li* is a measure equal to about one third of a mile. The distance across the Atlantic Ocean is about thirty-five hundred miles. On one of Cheng Ho's voyages, made about twenty years before Columbus was born, the Chinese explorer traveled as far as the east African city of Malinda, forty-five hundred miles from Beijing.

Joseph R. Levenson, ed., *European Expansion and the Counter-Example of Asia 1300–1600* (Englewood Cliffs, NJ: Prentice-Hall, 1967), p. 15.

Since the buildings of the Forbidden City were constructed of wood, the buildings you see today are mostly reconstructions of earlier Ming buildings, though the Grand Ancestral Shrine was last rebuilt in 1464, after a fire.

page 47 Nearly every country considers itself to be the center of the earth. Look at maps of the world printed in the United States and note where the Americas are located.

The Great Wall (or Long Wall) of China is the only human-made structure that can be seen from outer space. It was built in the Qin dynasty (221–206 B.C.) and rebuilt and extended by later Chinese rulers. The purpose of the wall was to protect China proper from nomadic northern tribes like the Mongols and the Manchus. It is nearly two thousand miles long.

The last Ming emperors relied on advisers to run the vast empire. In 1449, one poor emperor was foolish enough to leave the Forbidden City and attempt to lead an army against a wily Mongol chieftain with an army half as large. The outnumbered Mongol horsemen destroyed the Chinese, and the emperor himself was taken captive and held for ransom. At the other extreme, a later Ming emperor shut himself up in his palace and devoted himself totally to self-cultivation under the tutelage of Taoist monks. He died, ironically, of an overdose of "longevity pills."

page 51 The present Gold Pavilion is a reconstruction of the original, which was burned down by a deranged young man in 1950.

page 52 W. Scott Morton, *Japan: Its History and Culture* (New York: Thomas Y. Crowell, 1970), p. 10.

page 57 At this time a system was devised to use Chinese characters to write Vietnamese. In the seventeenth century a phonetic Vietnamese written language was invented by Roman Catholic missionaries.

page 60 To read more about Hinduism, see the National Geographic Society's 1971 book *Great Religions of the World*. This quotation was taken from page 34 of that book.

page 61 The Hindu caste system divided society into four major hereditary groups. Each group was restricted to certain occupations, and intermarriage between castes was banned. Certain persons were declared outcastes or "untouchables." These people were forbidden to use the public roads, for fear their shadows might fall on a superior and thus pollute the higher person. In recent years laws have been passed to make life more bearable for outcastes and many of the damaging extreme customs and beliefs of the caste system have been moderated.

page 65 Calicut is the ancient name for the modern city of Kozhikode, located in Kerala Province.

Perhaps the greatest dynasty of India was yet to come. This dynasty was known as the Mughal (a word related to Mongol, although the Mughal rulers were not pure Mongol in ancestry). Of the Mughal emperors, the greatest was Asbar (1556–1605). He himself was Muslim, but he respected Hindu religion and culture and is remembered for his political wisdom and his enlightened and humane treatment of his subjects.

Africa

page 67 In 1960, discoveries in the Olduvai Gorge in Kenya, east Africa, made by Dr. L. S. B. Leakey and his wife, Mary Leakey, were among the first to show that *Homo habilis,* a direct ancestor of *Homo sapiens* (modern humans), lived in Africa millions of years ago.

page 69 In *Introduction to African Civilizations* (1970), John G. Jackson uses the Edfu Text, a famous inscription on the Temple of Horus in Egypt, to support his theory that people migrated into Egypt from south to north, beginning in about 5000 B.C. These people, according to Jackson, "possessed tools and weapons of iron . . . and brought with them a well-developed civilization" (pages 93–94).

A contemporary writer, Stanley Lane-Poole, wrote about what happened to Spain after the Moors left. "For a while Christian Spain shone, like the moon with a borrowed light; then came the eclipse. . . . The land, deprived of the skillful irrigation of the Moors, grew impoverished and neglected; the richest and the most fertile valleys languished and were deserted; most of the populous cities . . . fell into ruinous decay; and beggars, friars and bandits took the place of scholars, merchants and knights. So low fell Spain when they had driven away the Moors . . ."

page 70 The head of the Muslim religion is called a caliph (KAY-lif), a word that means "successor" or "representative of Muhammad."

When Muhammad the Prophet died, his father-in-law, Abu Bekr, was elected caliph. But others believed the prophet's brother-in-law, Ali, should have become caliph by right of heredity. The religion split along lines of leadership: those who followed Abu Bekr were called Sunni Muslims, and those who followed Ali were called Shiite Muslims.

Muslim conquerors were often blamed for the destruction of the great library in Alexandria, Egypt. Actually the library was first destroyed in 48 B.C. by Julius Caesar's invading army. Mark Antony had it restored, but it was destroyed again by Christian monks in A.D. 387 (Jackson, page 121).

page 77   Jackson quotes historian Harold G. Lawrence from *African Exploration of the New World*.

> That Africans voyaged across the Atlantic before the era of Christopher Columbus is no recent belief. Scholars have long speculated that a great seafaring nation which sent its ships to the Americas once existed on Africa's west coast. . . . We can now positively state that the Mandingoes of the Mali and Songhay Empires, and possibly other Africans, crossed the Atlantic to carry on trade with the Western Hemisphere Indians, and further succeeded in establishing colonies throughout the Americas.

African historian and writer Basil Davidson wrote in his article "Africans Before Columbus?" (*West Africa* no. 2714, Saturday, June 7, 1969),

> The view that Mansa Muhammad's expeditions were a figment of Mansa Musa's imagination, or that, if they really did take place, they altogether failed to reach the Americas, has thus to overlook a great many bits of and pieces of evidence to the contrary. This evidence has been largely set aside by historians, one cannot help feeling, because of some inherent preconception about the inability of Africans to navigate at sea. . . . Medieval Mali was no mere outpost of the civilised world . . . it was in touch with the eastern world of Islam through many travellers and learned men, and the eastern world of Islam was very familiar with the sea. Travelling was very much in the spirit of West Africa, then as later; and if by land, why not by sea as well?

For further reading on the subject of African exploration in the New World prior to Columbus, see books and articles written by African historians Ivan Van Sertima, Basil Davidson, Stanlake Samkange, and J. Desmond Clark.

page 79   Their nomadic way of life and the Islamic religion combined to create the rugged Berber philosophy, reflected in one of their folk proverbs: "If you are a peg, endure the knocking; if you are a mallet, strike!" If a person was caught stealing from one of his own, his hand was cut off. The sick and severely injured were left behind if they weren't ready to move when camp broke. If they survived, it was "the will of Allah." If they died, that was the will of Allah, too. As the Berber saying goes, "The world has not promised anything to anybody."

page 82   Basil Davidson dismissed history books that suggested the east African cities were Persian or Arabian in his book *Africa in History* (New York: Macmillan, 1974). "History books saying this are out of date and they are wrong. . . . People who have studied these cities on the East Coast say that the cities were an important part of Africa's life between the years 1000 and 1700. And these cities were African, or to be more exact, Swahili."

page 90 The Benin hunters killed elephants for food. The ivory tusks were a bonus of the hunt. Later, the African elephant was hunted exclusively for its tusks, its body left to rot. Today elephants are considered a threatened species and their herds are protected by law.

page 92 Europeans didn't introduce slavery to Africans. Slavery had existed in various forms. But the contributing authors and editors of *The Horizon History of Africa* (New York: American Heritage Publishing Company, 1971) agree that "a slave in any African society was treated as a human being who could own property, marry, have children. . . . Had the kings and chiefs been aware of the enormity of the difference in the status of a slave in their own society and in the society of the New World, they probably would have put up greater and more sustained resistance."

The Americas

page 129 "*Tihui . . .*" Alfonso Caso, *The Aztecs: People of the Sun* (Norman: University of Oklahoma Press, 1958).

page 153 Columbus was distressed when he learned that some of the people of the islands ate human flesh, and he called such people *cannibals*—which was a distortion of the word Caribbean.

BIBLIOGRAPHY

Europe

ARIÈS, PHILIPPE, and GEORGES DUBY, eds. *A History of Private Life*. Vol. 2, *Revelations of the Medieval World*. Cambridge, MA: Harvard University Press, 1988.

ASTON, MARGARET. *The Fifteenth Century: The Prospect of Europe*. New York: Harcourt Brace, 1968.

BOORSTIN, DANIEL J. *The Discoverers: A History of Man's Search to Know His World and Himself*. New York: Random House, 1983.

CARDINI, FRANCO. *Europe 1492*. New York: Facts on File, 1989.

DURANT, WILL. *The Renaissance: A History of Civilization in Italy, 1304–1576*. New York: Simon & Schuster, 1953.

FERNANDEZ-ARNESTO, FELIPE. "Columbus and the Conquest of the Impossible." *Saturday Review*, 1974.

———. *Columbus*. Oxford: Oxford University Press, 1991.

GAIL, MARZIEH. *Life in the Renaissance*. New York: Random House, 1968.

HARLEY, J. B. *Maps and the Columbian Encounter*. Madison, WI: University of Wisconsin Press, 1990.

JAFFE, IRMA B., VIOLA GIONNI, FRANCO ROVIGATTI, eds. "Imagining the New World: Columbus Iconography." *Encyclopedia Italiana*, 1991.

LEVENSON, JAN, ed. *Circa 1492*. New Haven: Yale University Press, 1991.

MORISON, SAMUEL ELIOT. *Admiral of the Ocean Sea*. Boston: Little, Brown, 1946.

ROEDER, RALPH. *Man of the Renaissance*. Garden City, NY: Doubleday, 1933.

ROWLING, MARJORIE. *Everyday Life in Medieval Times*. New York: Putnam, 1948.

SMITH, DENIS. *Medieval Society, 800–1713*. New York: Dorset Press, 1968.

TREVALYN, G. M. *Illustrated History of England*. New York: David McKay, 1926.

Asia

ARNOLD, GUY. *Datelines of World History*. New York: Warwich Press, 1983.

BENOIST-MECHIN, JACQUES. *Arabian Destiny*. Translated by Denis Weaver. Fair Lawn, NJ: Essential Books, Inc., 1958.

BONAVIA, JUDY. *The Silk Road*. Secaucus, NJ: Chartwell Books, Inc., 1988.

BOORSTIN, DANIEL J. *The Discoverers: A History of Man's Search to Know His World and Himself*. New York: Random House, 1983.

BRYCE, L. WINIFRED. *India: Land of Rivers*. Camden, NJ: Thomas Nelson and Sons, 196

BUEHR, WALTER. *The World of Marco Polo*. New York: G. P. Putnam's Sons, 1961.

CADY, JOHN F. *Thailand, Burma, Laos, and Cambodia*. Englewood Cliffs, NJ: Prentice-Hall, 1966.

CARDINI, FRANCO. *Europe 1492*. New York: Facts on File, 1989.

CHAMBERS, JAMES. *The Devil's Horsemen*. New York: Atheneum, 1979.

FAIRSERVIS, WALTER A., JR. *India*. New York: World Publishing Co., 1961.

FITZGERALD, C. P. *China: A Short Cultural History*. New York: Praeger, 1961.

GOLDSCHMIDT, ARTHUR, JR. *A Concise History of the Middle East*. Boulder: Westview Press, 1991.

GROUSSET, RENÉ. *Conqueror of the World: The Life of Chingis-Khan*. Translated by Marian McKellar and Denis Sinor. New York: Orion Press, 1966.

———. *The Empire of the Steppes: A History of Central Asia*. Translated by Naomi Walford. New Brunswick, NJ: Rutgers University Press, 1970.

HAMMER, ELLEN. *Vietnam: Yesterday and Today*. New York: Holt, Rinehart and Winston, Inc., 1966.

KEENE, DONALD, comp. and ed. *Anthology of Japanese Literature*. New York: Grove, 1960.

KINROSS, LORD. *The Ottoman Centuries*. New York: Morrow Quill, 1977.

LAMB, HAROLD. *Ghenghis Khan and the Mongol Horde*. Hamden, CT: Linnet Books, 1990 (reprint from 1954).

LAPIDUS, IRA M. *A History of Islamic Societies*. Cambridge: Cambridge University Press, 1988.

LEVENSON, JOSEPH R., ed. *European Expansion and the Counter-Example of Asia 1300–1600*. Englewood Cliffs, NJ: Prentice-Hall, 1967.

MAJOR, JOHN S. *The Land and People of Mongolia*. New York: Lippincott, 1990.

MELTZER, MILTON. *Columbus and the World Around Him*. New York: Watts, 1990.

MILLARD, ANNE, and FRANCES HALTON. *Atlas of World History*. New York: Warwick Press, 1982.

MODAK, MANORAMA R. *The Land and the People of India*. Philadelphia: Lippincott, 1960.

MORTON, W. SCOTT. *Japan: Its History and Culture*. New York: Thomas Y. Crowell, 1970.

MOSHER, GOUVERNEUR. *Kyoto: A Contemplative Guide*. Rutland, VT: Tuttle, 1964.

MUNSTERBERG, HUGO. *The Arts of Japan: An Illustrated History.* Rutland, VT: Tuttle, 1957.

NATIONAL GEOGRAPHIC SOCIETY. *Great Religions of the World.* Washington, D.C.: National Geographic Society, 1971.

———. *Journey into China.* Washington, D.C.: National Geographic Society, 1982.

NEWMAN, ROBERT. *The Japanese: People of the Three Treasures.* New York: Atheneum, 1964.

POLO, MARCO. *The Travels of Marco Polo.* New York: Orion Press, n.d.

REISCHAUER, EDWIN O., and JOHN K. FAIRBANK. *East Asia: The Great Tradition.* Boston: Houghton Mifflin, 1960.

SANSOM, GEORGE. *A History of Japan 1334–1615.* Stanford: Stanford University Press, 1961.

SCHULBERG, LUCILLE. *Historic India: The Great Ages of Man.* New York: Time-Life Books, 1968.

SEEGER, ELIZABETH. *The Pageant of Chinese History.* New York: Longmans, Green and Co., 1947.

SMITH, BRADLEY, and WAN-GO WENG. *China: A History in Art.* New York: Doubleday Windfall, 1979.

SPENCER, WILLIAM. *The Land and People of Turkey.* Philadelphia: Lippincott, 1958.

VLAHOS, OLIVIA. *Far Eastern Beginnings.* New York: Viking, 1976.

WATSON, FRANCIS. *A Concise History of India.* New York: Charles Scribner's Sons, 1975.

WOLPERT, STANLEY. *A New History of India.* New York: Oxford University Press, 1989.

Africa

BASSANI, EZIO, and WILLIAM B. FAGG. *Africa and the Renaissance: Art in Ivory.* New York: Center for African Art and Prestel-Verlag, 1988.

BENNETT, LERONE. *Before the Mayflower—A History of Black America.* Chicago: Johnson Publishing Company, Inc., 1987.

BOYD, HERB. *African History for Beginners.* New York: Writers and Readers Publishing, Inc., 1991.

BROWN, LESLIE. *Africa: A Natural History.* New York: Random House, 1960.

CHU, DANIEL, and ELLIOTT SKINNER. *The Glorious Age in Africa:* Garden City, NY: Doubleday Publishing Company, 1965.

COUGHLAN, ROBERT, et al. *Tropical Africa.* New York: Time-Life Incorporated, 1966.

DAVIDSON, BASIL. *The African Genius.* Boston: Little, Brown and Company, 1969.

———. "Africans Before Columbus?" *West Africa* 2714 (June 7, 1969).

———. *A History of East and Central Africa.* New York: Doubleday Anchor Books, 1969.

———. *The Lost Cities of Africa.* Boston: Little, Brown and Company, 1987.

———, ed. *The African Past.* New York: Universal Books, Grosset & Dunlap, 1967.

DAVIDSON, BASIL, et al. *African Kingdoms.* With an introduction by Roland Oliver. New York: Time-Life Books, 1971.

FAGE, J. D. *A History of West Africa.* Cambridge: Cambridge University Press, 1969.

FLAUM, ERIC. *Discovery: Exploration Through the Centuries.* New York: W. H. Smith Publishers, Inc., 1990.

FLINT, JOHN E. *Nigeria and Ghana.* Englewood Cliffs, NJ: Prentice-Hall, 1966.

JACKSON, JOHN G. *Introduction to African Civilizations.* With an introduction and additional bibliographical notes by John Nenrik Clarke. New York: Carol Publishing Group, 1970.

JEFFERSON, E. *History of African Civilization.* New York: Thomas Y. Crowell Company, 1972.

JOSEPHY, ALVIN M., JR., ed. *The Horizon History of Africa.* New York: American Heritage Publishing Company, 1971.

KINDER, HERMANN, and WERNER HILGEMANN. *The Anchor Atlas of World History.* Vol. 1: *From the Stone Age to the Eve of the French Revolution.* New York: Doubleday Anchor Books, 1964.

KOLOSS, HANS-JOACHIM. *Art of Central Africa: Masterpieces from the Berlin Museum für Volkerkunde.* New York: Metropolitan Museum of Art, 1990.

MOUNTFIELD, DAVID. *A History of African Exploration.* Northbrook, IL: Domus Books, 1976.

OLIVER, ROLAND. *The African Experience.* New York: HarperCollins 1991.

OLIVER, ROLAND, and J. D. FAGE. *A Short History of Africa.* New York: Penguin Books, 1990.

RODINSON, MAXIME. *The Arabs.* Translated by Arthur Goldhammer. Chicago, IL: University of Chicago Press, 1981.

ROSENTHAL, RICKY. *The Splendor That Was Africa.* Dobbs Ferry, NY: Oceana Publications, Inc., 1967.

"The Search for Columbus." *National Geographic* 181, no. 1 (1992).

SEGY, LADISLAS. *Masks of Black Africa.* New York: Dover Publications, Inc., 1976.

SHUNNUE, MARGARET. *Ancient African Kingdoms.* New York: St. Martin's Press, 1965.

VAN SERTIMA, IVAN. *They Came Before Columbus: The African Presence in Ancient America.* New York: Random House, 1976.

WALLIS, FRANK. *Ribbons of Time—A World History Year by Year Since 1492.* New York: Weidenfeld and Nicolson, 1988.

WILLETT, FRANK. *African Art.* New York: Praeger Publishing Company, 1971.

Australia and Oceania

ABBIE, A. A. *The Original Australians.* Balgowah, Australia: Reed Books.

"Australian Aboriginal Culture." Australian Government Publishing Service, 1924.

BAGLIN, DOUGLASS, and DAVID MOORE. *The Dark Australians.* Australia and New Zealand Book Company, 1970.

BEAGLEHOLE, J. C. *Exploration of the Pacific.* 3d ed. 1966.

CRAIG, ROBERT D., and FRANK P. KING. *Historical Dictionary of Oceania.* Westport, CT: Greenwood Press, 1981.

FRYER, DONALD W., and JAMES C. JACKSON. *Indonesia.* Ernest Benn Ltd., 1977.

LEWIS, DAVID. *From Maui to Cook: The Discovery and Settlement of the Pacific.* New York: Doubleday, 1977.

LOVERING, J. F., and J. R. V. PRESCOTT. *Last of Lands . . . Antarctica.* Victoria: Melbourne University Press, 1979.

ORBELL, MARGARET. *The Natural World of the Maori.* New York Collins, 1985.

RABLING, HAROLD. *Pioneers of the Pacific: The Story of the South Seas.* London: Angus and Robertson, 1965.

SINCLAIR, KEITH, ed. *The Oxford Illustrated History of New Zealand.* Oxford: Oxford University Press, 1990.

The Americas

ANGIER, NATALIE. "A 'Lost City' Revisited." *Time* magazine, February 11, 1985.

BANCROFT-HUNT, NORMAN. *The Indians of the Great Plains.* New York: Morrow, 1982.

BANKS, GEORGE. *Peru Before Pizarro.* Oxford, 1977.

BELTRAN, MIRIAM. *Cuzco: Window on Peru.* New York: Knopf, 1970.

BENNETT, WENDELL. *Ancient Arts of the Andes.* New York: Museum of Modern Art, 1955.

BERNAL, IGNACIO. *Mexico Before Cortez.* Garden City, NY: Anchor Doubleday, 1975.

BLISH, HELEN H. *A Pictographic History of the Oglala Sioux: Drawings by Amos Bad Heart Bull.* Lincoln: University of Nebraska Press, 1967.

Book of the Chilam Balam of Chumayel. Translated and annotated by Ralph L. Roys. From first edition by the Carnegie Institution of Washington, D.C., 1933. Norman, 1967.

BURLAND, COTTIE. *North American Indian Mythology.* New York: P. Bedrick, 1985.

———. *Peoples of the Sun.* London: Weidenfeld and Nicolson, 1976.

CANBY, THOMAS Y. "The Search for the First Americans." *National Geographic,* vol. 156, no. 3 (September 1979).

CASO, ALFONSO. *The Aztecs: People of the Sun.* Norman: University of Oklahoma Press, 1958.

CASSON, LIONEL, ROBERT CLAIBORNE, BRIAN FAGAN, and WALTER KARP. *Mysteries of the Past.* New York: Simon & Schuster, 1977.

CASTRO LEAL, MARCIA. *El Juego de Pelota: The Ball Game.* Mexico City, 1973.

CIEZA DE LEON, PEDRO DE. *The Incas.* Translated by Harriet de Onis; edited, with an introduction by Victor Wolfgang von Hagen. (Original publication: Seville, 1553.) Norman: University of Oklahoma Press, 1959.

CLAIBORNE, ROBERT. *The First Americans.* New York: Time-Life Books, 1973.

COE, MICHAEL D. *The Maya.* London: Thames and Hudson, 1980.

———. *Mexico.* London, 1962 (revised edition, New York: Thames and Hudson, 1984).

DOUGLAS, FREDERIC H., and RENÉ D'HARNONCOURT. *Indian Art of the United States.* New York: Museum of Modern Art, 1941.

DUNN, DOROTHY. *Plains Indian Sketch Books of Zo-Tom and Howling Wolf: 1877.* Flagstaff, 1969.

FARB, PETER. *Man's Rise to Civilization.* New York: Dutton, 1968, 1978.

GALLENKAMP, CHARLES. *Maya: The Riddle and Rediscovery of a Lost Civilization.* New York: D. McKay Co., 1976.

GOODMAN, JEFFREY. *American Genesis.* New York: Summit, 1981.

GRAHAM, JOHN A., ed. *Ancient Mesoamerica: Selected Readings.* Palo Alto: Peek Publications, 1981.

GUAMAN POMA DE AYALA, FELIPE. *Letter to a King: A Peruvian Chief's Account of Life Under the Incas and Under Spanish Rule.* Translated, arranged, and edited by Christopher Dilke from *Nueva Coronicay Buen Gobierno,* written 1567–1615; original manuscript held by The Royal Library of Copenhagen. New York: Dutton, 1978.

HABERLAND, W. *The Art of North America.* New York: Crown, 1964.

HAGEN, VICTOR W. VON. *The Aztec: Man and Tribe.* New York: New American Library, 1958.

———. *Realm of the Incas.* New York: New American Library, 1961.

HAINES, FRANCIS. *The Plains Indians.* New York: Thomas Y. Crowell, 1976.

HALL, ALICE J. "A Traveler's Tale of Ancient Tikal." *National Geographic,* vol. 148, no. 6 (December 1975).

HEMMING, JOHN. *Machu Picchu.* New York: Newsweek, 1981.

HIGHWATER, JAMAKE. *Arts of the Indian Americas: Leaves from the Sacred Tree.* New York: Harper & Row, 1983.

———. *Journey to the Sky: The Rediscovery of the Maya.* New York: Thomas Y. Crowell, 1978.

———. *The Sun, He Dies.* New York: Lippincott & Crowell, 1980.

JENISON, MADGE. *Roads.* Garden City, NY: Doubleday, 1948.

LANNING, EDWARD P. *Peru Before the Incas.* Englewood Cliffs, NJ: Prentice-Hall, 1967.

LATHRAP, DONALD W. *Ancient Ecuador: Culture, Clay, and Creativity—3000–300 B.C.* Chicago, 1975.

LEONARD, JONATHAN NORTON. *Ancient America.* New York: Time-Life Books, 1967.

LEON-PORTILLA, MIGUEL. *Time and Reality in the Thought of the Maya.* Boston: Beacon, 1973.

MCINTYRE, LOREN. *The Incredible Incas and Their Timeless Land.* Washington, D.C.: National Geographic Society, 1975.

MEYER, KARL E. *Teotihuacán.* New York: Newsweek, 1973.

NICHOLSON, IRENE. *Mexican and Central American Mythology.* London: Hamlyn, 1967.

ORTIZ, ALFONSO, ed. *Handbook of North American Indians: Southwest.* Vol. 9. Washington, D.C.: Smithsonian Institution, 1979.

OSBORNE, HAROLD. *Indians of the Andes: Aymaras and Quechuas.* London: Routledge and Kegan Paul, 1952.

———. *South American Mythology.* London: Hamlyn, 1968.

PETERSEN, KAREN DANIELS. *Howling Wolf.* Palo Alto, 1968.

———. *Indians Unchained: Plains Indian Art from Fort Marion.* Norman: University of Oklahoma Press, 1970.

Popol Vuh: The Great Mythological Book of the Ancient Maya. Translated and with an introduction by Ralph Nelson. Boston: Houghton Mifflin, 1976.

Popol Vuh: The Sacred Book of the Ancient Quiche Maya. English version by Delia Goetz and Sylvanus G. Morley from the translation of Adrian Recinos. Norman: University of Oklahoma Press, 1950.

PRESCOTT, WILLIAM H. *The Conquest of Mexico* [1843]. Republished, New York, 1943.

PROSKOURIAKOFF, TATIANA. *An Album of Maya Architecture.* Norman: University of Oklahoma Press, 1963.

RENFREW, COLIN. *Before Civilization.* London: Jonathan Cape, 1973.

RUZ LHUILLIER, ALBERTO. *La civilización de los antiguos Mayas.* Mexico City, 1963.

SEJOURNE, LAURETTE. *Burning Water: Thought and Religion in Ancient Mexico.* Boulder, CO: Shambhala, 1976.

SILVERBERG, ROBERT. *Mound Builders of Ancient America.* Greenwich: New York Graphic Society, 1968.

SODI MORALES, DEMETRIO. *The Maya World.* Mexico City, 1976.

SOUSTELLE, JACQUES. *The Olmecs: The Oldest Civilization in Mexico.* Garden City, NY: Doubleday, 1984.

STUART, GEORGE E. "Who Were the 'Mound Builders'?" *National Geographic,* vol. 142, no. 6 (December 1972).

STUART, GEORGE E., and GENE S. STUART. *Discovering Man's Past in the Americas.* New York, 1969.

———. *The Mysterious Maya.* Washington, D.C.: National Geographic Society, 1977.

SUPREE, BURTON, and ANN ROSS. *Bear's Heart: Scenes from the Life of a Cheyenne Artist of One Hundred Years Ago with Pictures by Himself.* Philadelphia: Lippincott, 1977.

SWANTON, JOHN R. *The Indians of the Southeastern United States.* Washington, D.C.: U.S. Government Printing Office, 1946.

———. *Indian Tribes of the Lower Mississippi Valley and Adjacent Coast of the Gulf of Mexico.* Washington, D.C.: U.S. Government Printing Office, 1911.

TAMARIN, ALFRED, and SHIRLEY GLUBOK. *Ancient Indians of the Southwest.* Garden City, NY: Doubleday, 1975.

THWAITES, REUBEN GOLD, ed. *The Jesuit Relations and Other Documents.* Vols. 75–78, *Travels and Explorations of the Jesuit Missionaries in New France—1669 to 1737.* Cleveland: Burrows Brothers Company, 1901.

TILLETT, LESLIE. *Wind on the Buffalo Grass.* New York: Thomas Y. Crowell, 1976.

TRIGGER, BRUCE G. "Cultural Unity and Diversity" in *Handbook of North American Indians: Northeast.* Vol. 15. Washington, D.C.: Smithsonian Institution, 1978.

VAN SERTIMA, IVAN. *They Came Before Columbus: The African Presence in Ancient America.* New York: Random House, 1976.

WAUCHOPE, ROBERT. *Lost Tribes and Sunken Continents.* Chicago: University of Chicago Press, 1962.

WEAVER, MURIEL PORTER. *The Aztecs, Maya, and Their Predecessors.* New York: Seminar Press, 1972.

INDEX

(Page numbers in *italic* refer to illustrations.)

ACKNOWLEDGMENTS

Patricia and Fredrick McKissack would like to thank Dr. Barbara Woods, Professor of African and African American Studies at St. Louis University, for her help.

The maps on pages 4, 34, 68, 99, and 128 were prepared by Matthew Van Fleet.

The photographs and reproductions of art in this book are from the following sources and are used with permission:

Art Resource, New York, pages 6, 15, 16 *left and right,* 19. The Asia Society, New York, pages 54, 57, 61, 64. Australian Information Service, New York, pages 121, 123, 125. Beinecke Rare Book and Manuscript Library, Yale University, page 26. The Bettmann Archive, New York, pages 2, 5 *top and bottom,* 17 *left,* 22, 24, 25, 28, 29, 31, 41, 133, 149. Culver Pictures, Inc., New York, pages 10, 12, 132. Dallas Museum of Art, pages 130–31. The Detroit Institute of Arts, page 47. Dixson Library, State Library of New South Wales, Sydney, page 119. Engel Collection, Rare Books and Manuscripts Library, Columbia University, page 36. Werner Forman Archive, London, pages 71, 78, 82 *left,* 83, 94, 105, 106, 117, 137. The Granger Collection, New York, pages 8, 11, 14, 17 *right,* 20, 70, 76, 90. Japan Information Service, New York, pages 49, 50. The Metropolitan Museum of Art, New York, pages 39, 63, 85, 87, 89. Museo de America, Madrid, pages 135, 136. Museum of the American Indian, New York, page 151. National Museum of African Art, Smithsonian Institution, page 75 (Jeffrey Ploskonka). National Museum of the American Indian, New York, page 142. Collection of the National Palace Museum, Taiwan, pages 35, 43, 44. The New York Public Library, pages 13, 39, 46, 72, 80, 91, 93, 138, 144. The Philadelphia Museum of Art, page 82 *right.* Photo Researchers, New York, pages 59 (George Holton), 102 (Helen and Frank Schreiber), 113 (George Holton), 141 (Gregory G. Dimijian), 147 (George Gerster). Royal Palace Library, Madrid, page 129. *Sailing Craft of Indonesia* by Adrian Horridge, Oxford University Press, page 101. University Museum, University of Pennsylvania, page 148. Victoria and Albert Museum, London, page 37.